# FINGERS ON BUZZERS

A Celebration of the
# GREAT BRITISH QUIZ

# FINGERS ON BUZZERS

## JENNY RYAN
## AND LUCY PORTER

jb

First published in the UK by John Blake Publishing
An imprint of The Zaffre Publishing Group
A Bonnier Books UK company
4th Floor, Victoria House
Bloomsbury Square,
London, WC1B 4DA
England

Owned by Bonnier Books
Sveavägen 56, Stockholm, Sweden

www.facebook.com/johnblakebooks
twitter.com/jblakebooks

First published in 2023 by John Blake Publishing

Hardback ISBN: 978-1-78946-683-6
Ebook ISBN: 978-1-78946-684-3
Audiobook ISBN: 978-1-78946-685-0

British Library Cataloguing-in-Publication Data:
A CIP catalogue record for this book is available from the British Library.

Design by www.envydesign.co.uk

Printed and bound in Great Britain by Clays Ltd, Elcograf S.p.A

1 3 5 7 9 10 8 6 4 2

Photo credit: Mirrorpix

Every reasonable effort has been made to trace copyright-holders of material
reproduced in this book, but if any have been inadvertently overlooked the publishers
would be glad to hear from them.

John Blake Publishing is an imprint of Bonnier Books UK
www.bonnierbooks.co.uk

*Lucy*:

1) Someone who shares a first name with the poet, Dickinson, who wrote 'Hope is the thing with feathers'.

(Emily)

2) Someone whose first name is also the most popular papal name.

(John)

3) Someone who shares a first name with singers named Hawkins from The Darkness and Hayward from The Moody Blues.

(Justin)

*Jenny*:

For Kevin Ryan, the original 'Quiz King Kevin' (sorry, Mr Ashman) – the creator of this particular quiz monster. And for Julia Ryan and Dan Brown, who have always encouraged and supported this quiz monster.

*Both of us*:

For Amanda, producer extraordinaire, the woman who gets this show on the road.

# Contents

Introduction                                    1

1. PURIST VS GIMMICK                           15

2. THE GENERATION GAMES                        45

3. ON YOUR BUZZERS                             67

4. A QUESTION OF SPORT                         89

5. SCREEN TEST                                107

6. POPMASTERS                                 119

7. THE STAR PRIZE                             135

8. MEAN QUIZZES                               153

9. JET SET                                    169

10. HOW TO HOST YOUR OWN QUIZ                 182

SUPER QUIZ                                    205

Answers                                       239

Acknowledgements                              263

# Introduction

Hello!

## WHO ARE WE?

We are Lucy Porter and Jenny Ryan, and together we host *Fingers on Buzzers*, the country's number one podcast about quizzing and quiz shows.

## WHY DID WE WRITE THIS BOOK?

We love quizzing – truly, madly and deeply – and we wanted to share the love. For Jenny, quizzing is her livelihood, and for Lucy, it's her number one hobby. We're also both obsessed with TV quizzes and game shows, and it turns out, so is most of the UK. So there is something for everyone in these pages.

## WHAT IS THIS BOOK?

We're going to look back at some of the greatest (and not so great) quiz shows of all time, and work out what made them so good (or not). And we'll use this information to give you ideas about how to host your very own game show at home – right now! (Perhaps not right now – please continue to read the book for a bit.)

We're big fans of a basic quick-fire question quiz, but there are so many other options out there if you're running a quiz for family, friends, colleagues or even your arch-nemeses. This book will provide inspiration and practical tips on making the best quiz for any event and any audience.

By the end of the book we'll have given you:

- Lots of quiz questions and game suggestions to try out on your friends and family

- Tips on how to write fun and exciting quizzes for any audience

- A whistle-stop tour through the history of quiz and game shows on TV (plus some warm, fuzzy, nostalgic feelings if you're old enough to remember some of them).

We've consulted trivia experts, professional question setters and some famous hosts to bring you great insider tips. We'll also be sharing personal anecdotes along the way. You'll discover the answers to burning questions such as:

- Who are the 'hundred people' from the phrase: 'We asked a hundred people . . .' on *Family Fortunes* and *Pointless*?

- What happened to the speedboats, cars and caravans that people won on *Bullseye*? (Spoiler: they sold them for cold, hard cash.)

- Where did the most successful contestants on Euro quiz smash hit *Going for Gold* come from? And why the hell did they agree to compete in their second or third language against professional British quizzers like Daphne Fowler?

- When and why did Dusty Bin from *3-2-1* get consigned to the rubbish heap? And can we resurrect him?

We may play a little fast and loose at times with the definition of a quiz show but, forgive us, we just love them all. Strictly speaking, all quiz shows are game shows, but not all game shows are quiz shows. We are pretty generous in what makes a quiz show: e.g. *Countdown* is just about a quiz – it just happens to ask the same three questions over and over again (What's the longest word you can make? Can you do this sum? What's this big anagram?) Panel shows also count, as long as there are a few questions with correct answers in the programme (so *QI* is in, but *Would I Lie To You?* is out).

## LUCY'S QUIZZING HISTORY

My dad was born in very modest circumstances in Northern Ireland ('we hadn't a pot to piss in' was his colourful description of his upbringing) and he worked incredibly hard to become a pharmacist. He eventually moved to Croydon, south London, and set up his own chemist's shop.

Dad was proud of his upward mobility, but when he mixed with other professional people, I think he felt a bit self-conscious about his background. He worked alongside doctors and other pharmacists who'd been privately educated, so he dedicated himself to learning in order to compete. I remember he was mortified when someone laughed at him for pronouncing 'archipelago' wrongly (he'd said it 'Archie Pelago' like it was someone's name, and he also pronounced 'hyperbole' like it was a US sports contest until the day he died).

My dad loved to watch quiz and game shows on TV. His favourites were *Bullseye* and *University Challenge*. He was a huge fan of comedy, especially Billy Connolly, Dave Allen and Victoria Wood. He also loved Bernard Manning, but nobody's perfect.

After dinner, my dad used to make us answer quiz questions in order to 'win' pudding. I've got a very sweet tooth, so I would swot up. Having to learn the capital of Peru* or the name of the Greek god of wine* seemed like a small price to pay for a slice of Arctic Roll or some Angel Delight (younger readers, ask your parents or grandparents about these culinary treats).

This love of trivia meant that I got picked for my primary

school quiz team, and at the age of 11 I glowed with pride when St Elphege's won the *Top of the Form* competition at our local community centre. The prize was a glass trophy, which I had to share with the other three team members, and we also got a digital watch apiece. I lost the digital watch years ago, but I can still feel the thrill of the victory – in your FACE Roundshaw Juniors!

In high school I was at best a fair to middling student. Last year (at the age of 49) I was diagnosed with ADHD, and it made sense of the struggles I had with concentrating on writing long essays or completing difficult coursework. I was always good at remembering random facts though, and I think that's why I gravitated towards quizzing.

I managed to get into the University of Manchester and would go to the legendary pub quiz at the Red Lion in Withington. It was attended by lecturers from the uni, and the standard was dizzyingly high. I would have given up on it altogether, because my team never had a chance of winning, but luckily the beer was cheap and we could go to the nearby Aladdin's kebab shop on the way home, so I stuck with it, and it taught me that some pub quizzes can be very academic.

I had inherited my dad's love of comedy, and I was lucky enough to live in Manchester in the mid-1990s when there was a new and exciting comedy scene. I got to see Caroline Aherne, Steve Coogan and John Thomson at the start of their careers, and I soon decided to give stand-up a go myself. Working nights made it hard to get to pub quizzes, but I still loved going home to see my parents and watch TV shows with them like *Fifteen to One* and *The Weakest Link*. My dad actually put in an application to be on *Fifteen to One*, but the week he was invited to audition he'd been scheduled for a hip replacement, so he chose physical flexibility over mental dexterity, and we'll never know what could have been.

My comedy career took off in the early 2000s, and I got to appear on panel games like *Never Mind the Buzzcocks*, *QI* and *Have I Got News for You*. These appearances let me show off some of my general knowledge, but I was mostly trying to prove I was funny rather than clever. Then, as my star began to rise in show business, I was invited to do the celebrity versions of quiz shows. This was when the keen, competitive side of me that I'd neglected since the heady days of St Elphege's Primary School began to re-emerge.

My turns on TV quiz shows have been some of my happiest and proudest moments. My dad lived to see me compete on *Fifteen to One*, alongside one of his comedy heroes (and fellow Northern Irishman) Frank Carson, as well as *The Weakest Link* and *Mastermind*. I appeared on the celebrity version of *The Chase*, and it was there that I met the flame-haired mega-brain Jenny Ryan and we conceived the idea for our podcast *Fingers on Buzzers*.

I'm still a touring stand-up, but I've managed to combine my twin loves of quizzing and comedy in our podcast, and I still do as many quiz shows as I possibly can. Recently, I was delighted to earn the title of *Celebrity Mastermind* 'Champion of Champions'. The victory was all the sweeter because my specialist subject was my dad's favourite – Victoria Wood. So I like to think that he would have been doubly proud.

I've also managed to raise thousands of pounds for causes that are close to my heart through my quizzing escapades. Whenever I go on a 'so-called-celebrity' (© anonymous internet people) quiz show, I feel the pressure to do well. Not just for the sake of my own ego and to honour my dad's memory, but because I know that the money I make can do so much good for charities and organisations that really need it.

When my mum was caring for my dad, and then when my sisters and I were looking after my mum, we had amazing support from Carers UK. My family and I have been personally indebted to the Edinburgh Sick Kids hospital and Action for Stammering Children, so I always try to mention them whenever I can. I consider it an absolute privilege to have a public platform from which to thank the charities that have touched my life so profoundly.

The charities I work with are grateful for the exposure that they get by being mentioned on a prime-time quiz show, and I'd love to say that I only reluctantly do these shows as a means to get these charities recognised. But, who am I kidding? I LOVE doing quizzes, and this is my absolute favourite way to raise money for charity! I'm sure my dad would approve.

*Lima

*Dionysus, but we will also accept Bacchus

## JENNY'S QUIZZING HISTORY

I was indoctrinated into the 'Great British cult of quizzing' at a very early age.

When folk ask me, 'How did you get into quizzing?', they don't tend to expect the answer to be that I was answering general knowledge questions before I could add up double-digit numbers, but that was my start in life.

Everyone in my family is a quizzer, to one extent or another, and that's down to one man – my grandfather, Kevin Ryan. It is to him I owe the genetic predisposition to soak up facts like a sponge, and the adoration of quiz shows which has trained my brain to spit out those facts as they are needed. He is the reason that no Ryan family gathering is complete without a quiz, and also the reason those quizzes get so competitive that every year we have to add in more specific and convoluted rules to prevent actual bloodshed.

Grandad had taken early retirement from teaching by the time I came along, and so in my pre-school days while Mum was out at work, I was his little shadow. I'd stand in the kitchen with him while he peeled endless potatoes. I'd sit on his knee and 'read' the paper with him. I'd lie on the rug and watch his favourite afternoon programmes – which amounted to daytime repeats of *Hill Street Blues* and whatever quiz show was on. Thus it began.

Grandad was a smart chap. Fed up of me asking him to read everything out loud to me, he taught me to read at the earliest opportunity, aged three. This, however, opened another can of worms – the more I read, the more things I wanted explaining to me. 'Grandad, where's Nigeria? What's a joss stick? Where do lamb chops come from?' So his next task was to teach this curious little mind how to look up facts in reference books (ah, those innocent days before the internet!) which both sated my quest for information and, incidentally, kept me quiet for hours on end. Or at least until *Fifteen to One* came on.

At school, I was baffled that none of my classmates were as well informed as I was. Wasn't Trivial Pursuit compulsory in their family homes, too? I recall writing charity quizzes which not only bamboozled the kids in my class but also the teachers – and this was after I had added in clues and made them 'extra easy'. It wasn't really until I got to university that it dawned on me that I was an outlier. I'd popped into the Student Union to take the try-out test for the Leeds *University Challenge* team – more in hope than expectation – and ended up walking on to the team with the second-highest score. Once in the studio, I realised there were two things in life I would love to do as a career – quizzing and television.

It would be a few years yet before I put those two together professionally. In the meantime, I applied for any quiz show going – *Mastermind*, *The Weakest Link*, the aforementioned *Fifteen to One* – and got myself entrenched in the local and national competitive quiz scenes. Eventually I got my foot in the door of telly and worked as a question writer and researcher on shows including *QI* and *The Weakest Link* – even a short contract writing questions for the pilot of a long-forgotten format called *The Chase* (whatever happened to that?).

But what I really fancied was being on the other side of the camera, appearing as a professional know-it-all and, frankly, showing off a bit. I even tried to become an Egghead, taking part in two series of *Are You An Egghead?* I was doing quite well until in series one I came up against Dave 'Tremendous Knowledge' Rainford (a much-loved quiz scene stalwart who would eventually become an Egghead himself) and then in series two I was bested by one Anne Hegerty, later our own 'Governess' on *The Chase*. I responded to the defeat by asking her to join my local quiz league team, and she accepted.

And good that she did so. Five years down the line, in early 2014, Anne took me to one side after a cup match and asked if I'd fancy auditioning to join the Chasers. The producers had asked for recommendations of good women quizzers to audition, and she had thought of me immediately. Thanks to Anne putting in a good word for me, I was invited to meet with the programme makers . . . I'd love to say it was a quick and easy process, but by necessity it was thorough and drawn-out – after all, they had to be sure the right person got the gig. I compare it to casting a new Doctor or companion in *Doctor Who*, or giving the Rovers Return a new landlady in *Coronation Street* – like *The Chase*, these are shows beloved by millions of viewers and it's a huge decision to add someone new to the mix. They had to be sure I was right for the job. So, after nearly nine months of tests, auditions and more tests, the baby Vixen was born, and my life changed forever.

Being a Chaser is absolutely the dream job, the role I was born for. It's led to so many great things – including meeting fellow quiz maniac Lucy Porter and starting *Fingers on Buzzers*. I know my grandad would be incredibly proud – and a little bit envious – that I am now a professional quizzer, the path he set me on when I was still a toddler. Grandad died when I was ten and left a huge hole in the family, not least when we play games and need a quizmaster and rule enforcer. I feel sad every day that he's not around to see this. He'd have loved it. This book is very much for him. The local paper published a piece about him following his death, under the headline 'Quiz King Kevin'. I hope I am doing the dynasty justice.

★ ★ ★

As you can see, we were indoctrinated into the cult of quiz at an early age. We've watched thousands of hours of TV quizzing and we've worked both behind and in front of the camera on quiz and game shows.

We like to say that this is a golden age of the television quiz. At any given teatime you can see *The Chase* and *Pointless* trending on social media (and *Countdown* if someone's spelled out a rude word). The BBC has given us 'Quizzy Mondays' where *Only Connect* flows seamlessly into *University Challenge*. There are record numbers of new quiz shows appearing, both home-grown formats and ideas from overseas.

Thanks to the internet, you can even see quiz shows from other countries' broadcasters. From the US, you can see how *Family Feud* compares to *Family Fortunes*, catch up on international versions of *Jeopardy!* (which is huge in other countries but for some reason never caught on in the UK) and you can even find the Nigerian version of *Deal or No Deal*, hosted by John Fashanu.

In order to help you host your own quizzes and games, we're going to unpack some of the elements that make a successful TV show. We're going to take these shows apart, see how they work, and see how they can help you with your own home quizzes.

The last few years have seen a boom in home quizzing thanks to the events of 2020 and beyond (let's not dwell on those) and there's a great appetite for new ways of hosting your own games. We'll try to help you come up with some innovative ways of asking timeless general knowledge questions, and new ways of framing perennially popular puzzles.

Our heartfelt wish is that this book will inspire you, dear reader, to do a number of things.

We'd love it if you felt moved to look out for episodes of the quiz shows we reference – either on the internet or on your TV.

YouTube is a bottomless treasure trove – just search any of the names of shows or hosts you vaguely remember or think you might like, and there's almost certain to be something that'll draw you down a rabbit hole of vintage telly. Talking Pictures TV – https://www.tptvencore.co.uk/ has a number of quizzes in among all kinds of other delights, and the good old BBC iPlayer contains quiz and game shows both old and new. Challenge TV has got us through many a bleak night in a hotel room on tour, and the streaming services of all the major broadcasters, like ITVX, My5 and Channel 4 will see you right for many of the old shows we mention, plus you might discover some new formats that will become future classics.

We'd also be delighted if you took the time to seek out live quizzes. The pub quiz is a British institution and a great way to meet people, improve your knowledge and support the beleaguered hospitality sector. There are quiz leagues all over the country – all over the world in fact, hello overseas readers! – and they're ideal for people who want to take their quizzing to the next level. A great place to start in the UK is https:// www.abql.org.uk/members/default.aspx

Most of all, we'd implore you to host and participate in quizzes at home. We were both lucky enough to be inculcated with a love of trivia by family members. Children have an innate thirst for knowledge. Who hasn't at some point asked their parents: 'Why is the sky blue?' 'Do dogs have belly buttons?' or 'Why can't I just eat biscuits for every meal?' To be honest, we've never found a satisfactory answer to the last one.

Sometimes, as adults, we get so busy focusing on the specific knowledge we need for our jobs, hobbies or life admin that we lose our curiosity about life in general. We forget to stop and smell the flowers. And then we forget to ask ourselves, 'Why do flowers smell anyway?' Clearly to attract pollinators. Did you know that there are around 400 different chemicals that go to make up the scent of a rose? And can I just mention that the Indonesian corpse flower or *Amorphophallus titanum* mimics the odour of rotting meat to attract insects which lay their eggs in corpses or feast on decaying flesh?

Through making our podcast, we've gained a deeper understanding of what goes into making a successful quiz or game show for TV and radio, so we'd like to share that with you. We've included some sample quizzes and questions, but this isn't primarily a quiz book, it's more of a leaping off point for you to create your own quizzes for friends and family. We hope you enjoy it. Don't forget to keep up with our podcast for more insights.

# PURIST vs GIMMICK

## AASMAH MIR ON *MASTERMIND*:

Aasmah Mir's specialist subject on *Mastermind* was 'The Novels of Hanif Kureishi'.

*'I wanted to choose something that was finite. So I thought, "OK, it's seven specific books. If I read the seven books and make some notes then it won't be a disaster." Whereas, if I'd said something that I love like, "The history of Celtic Football Club," I would have got something wrong and then everyone would have said, "Well, you're not a proper Celtic fan are you?" So you don't actually do your favourite thing in life, you should do something that you think you can revise.'*

You can go low tech or high tech, involve physical challenges, feats of memory, forfeits and penalties. But to start with, let's take a look at some TV favourites to ask a fundamental question: what kind of quiz do you like?

If quizzes were pizzas, would you go for the simple pleasure of a Margherita, or would you fly in the face of tradition and pop pineapple on your Hawaiian? If quizzing was a cocktail bar would you be sitting in the corner sipping a single malt whisky, or would you be dancing on the table with a porn star Martini? Maybe you're gluten intolerant and teetotal and this is all a bit baffling to you, so we'll ask it plainly: are you a quiz purist, or do you love a bit of a gimmick?

There are broadly two types of quiz show: the ones where it's mostly about the questions, and the ones where it's mostly about the format – the 'gimmick' if you will. Purist or gimmicky, there is a place for all of them in our hearts here at *Fingers on Buzzers*.

## PURIST AND SIMPLE

At the heart of it, the purist quiz is all about the best quizzer winning by answering lots of lovely juicy questions. There may be a novel hook to the format, there may (or may not) be a huge prize to win, but when all is said and done, the real star of the show is the quiz itself.

---

## *MASTERMIND*
## Fact File

**NAME:** *Mastermind* (with many spin-offs and variations, see below)

**DATES:** The first iteration was on BBC1 from 1972 to 1997, then things all got a bit complicated until it came back properly on BBC2 from 2003 to the present day.

---

**HOSTS:** Most notably, Magnus Magnusson, John Humphrys and Clive Myrie. But oh boy, there are lots of others from the 'complicated' era including Des Lynam, Clive Anderson and Peter Snow. There were sports versions, Welsh language versions, one-off specials, a series for the Discovery Channel, some shows for Radio 4 and even a *Hip Hop Mastermind* featuring John Humphrys hosting, with Lethal Bizzle, DJ Semtex, DJ Target and A. Dot in the chair.

**PRIZE:** The series winner gets a glass bowl, engraved on a copper wheel by Denis Mann from the beautiful town of Wick in Caithness, Scotland. He's been making the winner's trophy since the very beginning of *Mastermind*, and every year Denis changes the design slightly.

**RULES:** Contestants compete in two timed rounds. Firstly on a specialist subject they've chosen, and secondly on general knowledge.

## MASTERMIND

The ultimate in back-to-basics quizzing. All you need is a chair, a spotlight and a large stack of fiendish trivia questions. Back in the day, they didn't even need a studio – original host Magnus Magnusson would pitch up at various academic locations around the nation to film the ritual interrogation of his victims – ahem – I mean willing contestants.

*Mastermind* is such a classic format, having run almost continually since 1972 (albeit hopping between broadcasters and even between television and radio) that it's surprising to learn it wasn't expected to be a smash hit, let alone a mainstay of schedules for decades. It originally went out in a late slot on Sunday nights, when viewership was low at the best of times. However, it got an unexpected promotion up the schedule thanks to none other than Leslie Phillips – well, hello! Phillips was the star of cheeky sitcom *Casanova '73*, which turned out to be far too racy for BBC viewers and, after complaints, it was bumped from its early evening time slot and replaced at the last moment with our favourite furniture-centric quiz show.

The simplicity of the format – two timed rounds per contestant, one on their specialist subject, one on general knowledge – is what makes it one of the most daunting shows for contestants. It's not for the faint of heart, because it's so exposing. Care must be taken when selecting your specialist subject. Do you choose something very niche, and expect deep-dive questions? Or a wider, broader topic and hope for more general queries? There's also an instinct to pick a topic that you love dearly – sure, you'll already know quite a bit about it, and you'll enjoy revising it . . . to begin with.

What if you get sick of it? Let's just say that *Buffy the Vampire Slayer* was my favourite show until I chose it as my specialist subject; I watched every episode three times before the recording, and I haven't watched it since. That was 2006.

## 🎤 HOST WITH THE MOST: Clive Myrie

*Mastermind* viewers are a loyal and devoted bunch, and any slight change to the set or the format can make waves – even a tweak of the timer graphic caused complaints to the BBC. It's quite lucky then that the hosts of the main show have had quite lengthy tenures.

Magnus Magnusson, the original host, was born in Iceland and raised in Edinburgh. He was a gentle and calming presence despite the inquisitorial nature of the show. His successor, Welshman John Humphrys, brought a little more urgency to the role during his lengthy run. He occasionally seemed to be hectoring hesitant contestants as if they were politicians on the *Today* programme, but he was much warmer and more twinkly than in his day job, and was clearly enjoying himself enormously.

New host Clive Myrie comes from a journalistic background, like his predecessors. As a BBC foreign correspondent he's covered global conflicts from Kosovo to Afghanistan.

But of course, his main strength is that, like all the best people, he comes from Bolton. We look forward to watching him for many years to come.

**OUR FAVOURITE . . .**

*MASTERMIND* WRONG ANSWER

On *Celebrity Mastermind* in 2020, actress Amanda Henderson was asked the following question:

'The 2019 book entitled *No One Is Too Small to Make a Difference* is a collection of speeches by a Swedish climate change activist. What is her name?'

Amanda tentatively answered: 'Sharon?'

The correct answer was Greta Thunberg, but people loved Amanda's answer, and the internet blew up immediately. Even Greta saw the funny side, and even changed the name on her Twitter profile to 'Sharon'. Amanda got such a hard time from the usual armchair geniuses on social media for giving what they considered a foolish answer, but we are here to tell you why it was actually genius.

In *Mastermind,* if you tie your score with another player, the player with the fewest passes is deemed to have won. You might save a few seconds by saying 'pass' (because if you get it wrong the quizmaster reads out the right answer), but we're not convinced that the time saving is worth the risk. Also, we all love to see a lucky guess pay off, so it's better to have answered and lost than never to have answered at all. We are firm believers that it is always worth venturing an answer. So, if you ever find yourself in the famous black chair and your mind wandering, just say whatever comes into your head.

# *FIFTEEN TO ONE*
# Fact File

**NAME:** *Fifteen to One*

**DATES:** 1988 to 2003, then 2013 to 2019

**HOSTS:** William G Stewart, Adam Hills, Sandi Toksvig

**PRIZES:** Very cool ancient artefacts. In the last grand final of the show in 1993, the leaderboard winner's prize was a decorated cup from the Greek colony in Apulia, southern Italy, dating from the fourth century BC. The grand prize was a black-figure *lekythos* made in Athens in the fifth century BC. (If you can tell us what a black-figure *lekythos* is, you deserve to win a prize too!) Legendarily, William G Stewart was a lover of antiquities, and spent part of a *Fifteen to One* episode in 1991 giving an impassioned speech about returning the marbles to the Parthenon.

**VITAL STATISTICS:** *Fifteen to One* was the first programme on British TV to claim the top five places in any channel's weekly top ten. In his 16 years as host, William G Stewart stood in front of the podium 2,265 times, welcomed 33,975 contestants and delivered just under 350,000 questions.

## FIFTEEN TO ONE

The questions are the stars of the show on the Channel 4 mainstay *Fifteen to One* (with a special mention to Laura, whose dulcet tones recapped the scores in the William G Stewart era). Very much the Thunderdome of quiz, in each episode 15 quizzers enter and one leaves. I mean, they all leave in a safe and orderly manner, but only one might make it into the grand final contested by the top 15 scorers across the entire series (which seemed to last all year).

To whittle the semi-circle of brains down, each contestant is asked a question in turn. Get your first two questions wrong – you're out. Get at least one right and it gets interesting – you're through to the third round of questions, in which a correct answer gives you the right to nominate an opponent to face the next one. This round almost qualifies *Fifteen to One* to count among the mean quizzes (see later in the book), as tactical nomination of either weaker or stronger opponents came into play, and factions among the contestants formed, eager to extinguish each podium's three lights indicating three lives.

The firm hand of original host William G Stewart on the tiller kept the nastiness at bay; WGS seemed to have little time for chat and kept the momentum of the show moving forward, always bringing the focus back to the questions. This was probably down to the fact that he had spent his career as a television producer and director; before his hosting stint he had helmed sitcoms such as *Father, Dear Father* and *The Rag Trade*, and game shows *Family Fortunes* and *The Price is Right*.

A man who knew the cost of studio time and the importance of format. And in fairness – he took legal action against 1997 series winner Trevor Montague, who had fibbed on his application by claiming he hadn't appeared on the show before.

The original run lasted from 1988 to 2003, and Channel 4 revived it ten years later with Sandi Toksvig hosting (with a touch more chat than WGS) plus Adam Hills taking charge of some celebrity specials. Off-air at the moment, it's a classic format that will be back.

## *UNIVERSITY CHALLENGE*
## Fact File

**NAME:** *University Challenge*
(Based on the American show named *College Bowl*)

**DATES:** 1962 to 1987 on ITV. The BBC revived it in 1994 and it continues to the present day.

**HOSTS:** Bamber Gascoigne, Jeremy Paxman, Amol Rajan Angus Deayton, Kirsty Wark and David Baddiel have hosted variations and spin-offs. Bamber Gascoigne has also been portrayed by Mark Gatiss in the movie *Starter for Ten*, and Griff Rhys Jones in *The Young Ones'* parody of the show.

**PRIZE:** A trophy. It may not seem much of a reward for the hours of study, but a purist quiz is never about the prizes.

And they do get cool people to come and hand over the goods. In 2017, Eric Monkman's Oxford Balliol team had their trophy presented by Stephen Hawking, and in 2023, historian and author Jung Chang handed the gong to the winning Durham side.

**CATCHPHRASES:**
'Your starter for 10'
'No conferring'

## UNIVERSITY CHALLENGE

Is *University Challenge* possibly the purest of purist quizzes? The *Mastermind* champion takes home an elegant glass bowl designed by Denis Mann; old-school series winners of *Fifteen to One* received an ancient artefact (although the revival changed this to a £40,000 cash prize). What do the series champions of *University Challenge* get? A trophy. Between four of them (five, including the reserve). Which they don't even get to keep – their academic institution gets dibs on displaying it.

If they're lucky, a *UC* contestant might get a spin-off show (e.g. Monkman and Seagull, with *Monkman and Seagull's Genius Guide to Britain*) or even end up as a professional quizzer (e.g. Leeds, Ryan, and Glamorgan, Labbett, whom you might know as Chasers). If they're unlucky, they might briefly become the subject of febrile articles in the press about their appearance (e.g. Corpus Christi, Oxford's Gail Trimble).

***********************************

**FUN FACT: So devoted to quizzing was Bamber Gascoigne, that when he went on Radio 4's *Desert Island Discs* in 1987, he let his wife choose the records without telling him what they were. He had to guess what she'd picked! It was like *Never Mind the Buzzcocks* meets *Mr & Mrs*.**

***********************************

ROGER TILLING ON *UNIVERSITY CHALLENGE*:
The very first episode of our podcast was called 'Roger Tilling's Milking Stool' because Roger described his set-up in the studio when he does the voiceover for *University Challenge*:

*'A lot of people think I'm pre-recorded, but I'm there. I sit on a milking stool in the corner and look for a light.'*

**HOST WITH THE MOST: Jeremy Paxman**

When *University Challenge* was revived in the 1990s, Paxman had a tough act to follow. Bamber Gascoigne had established the format in the UK and was so devoted to it that he even rewrote the questions himself, so that he was 100 per cent confident of the answers.

Paxman claimed that when he was approached to host the revival, he initially turned it down because it was so clearly

Bamber Gascoigne's show. Paxo only accepted the role when he heard from Bamber himself that he didn't want to do it.

Paxman went for a very different approach – where Bamber had been encouraging and pally with the students, Paxo was, well, not that. He could be incredibly grumpy. Even *UC* legend Eric Monkman felt his wrath, when Jeremy roared at him, 'That's a useless answer!' Even if you got a question right that didn't guarantee an easy ride. One Cambridge college answered a question before Jeremy had finished asking it and he called them 'smart arses'. He was clearly delighted when they got the next one wrong, crowing, 'See, they're not all so easy, are they?'

Like a brilliant professor or a distant father, he could be disdainful and downright rude at times, but you could sense that he only did it because he cared and wanted the young people to succeed. When he rolled his eyes and said, 'OH, COME ON!', it came from a place of love.

## YOU GOTTA HAVE A GIMMICK

On the other hand, some quiz shows make their unique mechanic or gimmick the focus of the format – with varying levels of success. We all enjoy a novelty, but some have more staying power than others. Who remembers the 2015 series *Freeze Out*, which combined quizzing with a sort of cross between curling and air hockey? Or *The Getaway Car*, a *Top Gear* spin-off with quiz questions and Dermot O'Leary? Well, quite. And let us never speak of 1990s cult quiz *Naked Elvis*.

Perhaps they concentrated too hard on the gimmick and not enough on the actual gameplay – unlike some of our longer-lived favourites.

## TIPPING POINT
## Fact File

**NAME:** *Tipping Point*

**DATES:** 2012 to present

**CONCEPT:** Answer questions, win counters, beat the machine!

**HOST:** The one and only Mr Ben Shephard

**PRIZES:** Theoretically, the top prize is £40,000, if you were lucky enough to score the jackpot and release both double counters. Often the winning contestant walks away with a decent cash prize (especially for a daytime show). If they're lucky they might bag one of the mystery prizes, which have included inflatable hot tubs, DJ decks and a year's subscription to a plant delivery service. The viewers are often critical of the quality of these spot prizes.

**JARGON:**
Rider
Ghost Drop
Ambient Drop

OWEN VISSER ON *TIPPING POINT*:
Owen was a contestant on *Tipping Point*, and he had a genius way of preparing for the pressure of being in the studio. Here is Owen's *Tipping Point* tip:

*'Once I knew I was going on, then I was in practice mode. At home with my girlfriend, I was playing a "tension bed" on the speakers and she was asking me general knowledge questions.'*

### 🎤 HOST WITH THE MOST: Ben Shephard

Vying with Les Dennis for the title 'nicest man in quiz', Ben is one of our absolute faves here at *Fingers on Buzzers*. He's incredibly sharp – with great general knowledge and tons of sports facts at his fingertips. He's a natural born presenter and the consummate professional quiz show host, but also incredibly kind when the players are let down by the machine, the counters or simply by themselves.

*Tipping Point* has become quite notorious for funny wrong answers. Ben regularly delivers a masterclass in keeping a straight face when a contestant is saying something spectacularly misguided.

The classic example of this was when two contestants wrestled with the question:

'In his epic poems, Homer often refers to nectar as the drink of the gods and which other substance as their food?'

The first contestant, Dom, confidently answered 'Donuts'. His opponent Lindsey backed him up: 'Yep, that's what Homer likes, beer and donuts!'

Then the penny dropped and Dom realised, 'I think I've mixed up my Homers,' which indeed he had. The correct answer was ambrosia in case you're wondering.

Lovely Ben didn't miss a beat and consoled Dom by saying, 'It's easy to mix up your Homers.' Bless.

BEN SHEPHARD, HOST OF *TIPPING POINT*:

*'I really want them all to win. I want them to go away with as much as possible. I want them to have a fantastic time, because I know if they've had a great time the show is probably going to be more watchable, and that's exciting . . . When we got a double jackpot winner I squealed like a kid. 'The* [Tipping Point] *machine has a name, which is a female name, but I'm not going to give it away! . . . She's a cruel mistress . . . I would urge anyone who comes in to be polite to the machine. It does seem like the machine does it on purpose; you can't help but take it personally.'*

## TIPPING POINT

For the first few years of *Tipping Point*'s existence, an oft-repeated snarky quip resounded around the UK. 'Can you believe they've made a whole game show based on the penny falls machine from the pier arcade?' folk guffawed, in a mildly snobbish tone. Until they watched the show, and found out that it was utterly compelling viewing.

The structure of the game (and most of the questions, in honesty) is very simple – pop counters into the giant machine, try to get more out than your opponents, and then in the final use the same method to knock the £10,000 jackpot chip out of the behemoth and into your bank account. What makes it so watchable is the hosting style of Ben Shephard, who has created a whole vocabulary around the game – rather like Noel Edmonds did on *Deal or No Deal*, but with less of the 'starting a cult' vibe.

Beware Ghost Drops (fast uncontrolled counter releases) and avoid the dreaded Riders (the released counter lands on top of one already in play) and contestants can not only win a lovely cash sum and mystery prizes, but, best of all, they get a Ben Shephard hug (six-star rating on Tripadvisor for hugs). For all its simplicity, *Tipping Point* has continued to draw in afternoon viewers for over a decade – take that, snobs! And it also continues to have me squawking at the screen when a finalist decides to put the Jackpot Counter in anything other than Zone 1 or 4.

## *100% Fact File*

**NAME:** *100%*

**DATES:** 1997 to 2001

**CONCEPT:** Answer 100 questions and score a higher percentage than your rivals.

**HOST:** Trick question! There wasn't one (well, it was Robin Houston, but we never saw him).

**PRIZE:** £100 and the chance to come back the next day – Ian Lygo managed to come back a whopping 75 times! He might have managed even more but the producers kicked him off, worried that viewers would get sick of the sight of him.

**FUN FACT:** There were occasionally special editions of the show with 100 questions about a single subject. Specials included Queen (the band) and Princess Diana (the princess). The Diana show was part of Channel 5's day of tribute programmes to the recently departed Princess of Wales. Some of the questions didn't seem that respectful: 'Michael Jackson wrote his song "Dirty Diana" about Diana. Is that true or false?' (The answer was false, thankfully.)

## 100%

What a gimmick – this was 'the game show without a host'! Well, sort of. You never saw question master Robin Houston on screen in *100%*, Channel 5's flagship quiz programme from its launch in 1997. There wasn't even any chit-chat between the contestants, other than their basic introductions. It was simply 100 multiple-choice questions fired out in succession, and the player with the highest percentage of correct answers played again the next day. It could easily have been classed as a purist quiz, but the slightly eerie and futuristic concept of automated quizzing makes this a great example of a gimmick quiz with staying power. We keenly await its revival, this time hosted by an actual AI chatbot.

★ ★ ★

## BORDERLINE CASES

*Only Connect* is an interesting format. Yes, there's lots of variety to the gameplay, with connections, sequences, missing vowels and – our favourite – the connecting walls. At heart though, it's a purist quiz, because it rewards very clever people for stuff they know, with no element of chance or requirement for physical dexterity. Again, crucially, there's no eye-popping sums of cash on offer, or swanky consumer goods, just another trophy that you have to share.

*Pointless* is another tricky one to categorise. Yes, there is money to be won, but not vast sums. The central gimmick – you have to guess the least popular answer – requires a layer of emotional intelligence on top of book smarts. Ultimately, we'd class it more at the purist end of the spectrum because it requires a decent level of general knowledge to do really well.

In a similar vein, *Jeopardy!* is a hard one to pin down. It has a gimmick, but it's been the same one for decades – you need to give the question, not the answer. There is big money on offer, but the huge winnings are only taken home by serious boffins.

If a quiz is too purist, there's a risk that viewers will find it dull or too difficult. If it's too gimmicky, it will alienate serious quiz fans. Find the sweet spot – you've got a hit on your hands.

## *POINTLESS*
## Fact File

**NAME:** *Pointless*

**DATES:** 2009 to present day

**HOSTS:** Alexander Armstrong and Richard Osman.

**PRIZE:** A cash jackpot which increases each week that it isn't won.

**CONCEPT:** Teams of two contestants answer a series of questions with answers which are not only correct, but also the most obscure. The aim of the final round being to provide an answer that no one else has given.

## *POINTLESS*

Richard Osman told us that he'd borrowed heavily from another show he'd produced – *Beat the Nation* – when he created *Pointless*. He said, 'You use parts of old shows sometimes to create new ones if you've got an idea that you know is good.'

In *Beat the Nation*, Tim Brooke-Taylor and Graeme Garden asked their contestants general knowledge questions which had previously been put to members of the public. The aim of the game was to answer questions that other people didn't know the answer to.

In *Pointless*, the difference is that members of the public have been asked a more general question like 'Name the top 30 wine-producing countries of the world'. As Alexander says on the show, 'We gave 100 people 100 seconds to name as many . . . as they could.' Because you get as many points as there were people who also said your answer, the trick is to find the least popular answers, ideally one that nobody else named, which is 'Pointless!'

So in our example of wine-producing countries, Spain, Italy and France would likely be high scorers. You'd be on safer ground with Chile or Hungary, and you'd be pretty unlucky if anyone else had said Moldova or Japan.

*Pointless* is not the only research-based game show – *Family Fortunes* and *8 Out of 10 Cats* spring to mind immediately – the twist is that here you're aiming to find the least popular things. It's been running since 2009 and the all-star edition started in 2011. The best thing about the celebrity version is that its title *Pointless Celebrities* really allows you to identify foolish people on social media. If anyone you know tweets 'Hah, yeah, well, this lot really are Pointless!' you immediately know you're best to cut off all ties with them. As if the producers of the show didn't spot that the title might be a bit insulting to their guests, but you, Mike from Northampton, are the first person to spot it.

## HOSTS WITH THE MOST: Alexander Armstrong and Richard Osman

Alexander is so charming and so funny. He's been a comedy actor, writer and Classic FM breakfast show host. He's knowledgeable but not smug with it. Warm with the contestants without being smarmy. He's posh but he doesn't wear red trousers.

Xander asks the questions and then Richard comes along and mops up the facts.

The double act with Richard works so well because it allows Xander to play along with the game, so he really is on the side of the contestants.

Richard is super smart and a bit playful, and the chemistry he has with Xander makes the show feel a little bit like an odd couple sitcom. He's now a massively best-selling author though, so he's allowing some guest co-hosts to sit in his big chair for a bit.

**LUCY SAYS:**

I was lucky enough to do a brief co-hosting stint on *Pointless*, which was an absolute dream. I can tell you that yes, Xander is as lovely as he seems. Also, Richard makes his job look easy, but that tall frame of his is clearly packed with facts.

What can we use from *Pointless* for our own quizzes?

Well, unless you're prepared to hire a market research organisation to ask 100 people questions for you, this could be tricky. If you're exceptionally popular you might have 100 friends you can ask. Or, you can go online and do some research yourself about what's popular and what's not.

For example, *Pointless* co-host Richard Osman launched the World Cup of Chocolate on his social media in 2016. So you could ask your contestants:

Can you name any of the four chocolates that made it to the final of WCOC in 2016? Clue: Three of them are bars, one comes in bags.

ANSWERS: Dairy Milk, Galaxy, Maltesers, Twirl.

## FORMAT YOUR OWN

'Let's have a quiz!' goes up the cry. Sure, you could get out a dusty old book of quiz questions and just ask them one by one, but that's going to get tiresome pretty rapidly. Consider your format – are you going to keep it purist and simple, or exploit a gimmick?

As always, it's a case of catering to your audience. Some people want a lot of questions, asked without too much fuss. In the 1980s, when Trivial Pursuit became a global phenomenon, in our house we quickly dispensed with the board and the little plastic pieces. (Did you call them wedges? Cheeses? Pies? Some weirdos apparently referred to them as pizza!) We just sat around firing off the questions from the cards. You could choose your own subject for one point, or answer in a category that someone else nominated for two points. It's a popular device in quizzing (see the home and away round in *A Question of Sport*) but adds a slight element of jeopardy.

If you've got a mixture of eggheads and jocks, you could borrow from *Bullseye* and give contestants different roles. Just like that show had 'knowers and throwers' you could have 'brainy and brawny'. We did a quiz once where one player had to lift another up, and the carried player could answer questions until the carrier could no longer bear their weight. One of you gets a mental workout, the other one gets a physical workout. Little tip from my experience here: do this over a soft surface, not on concrete. My husband dropped me quite spectacularly and I was left with a sore leg for days.

Even if you're planning a straightforward, pub-quiz style event, it's important to give it a bit of texture and variety. There's a reason why ten questions has become a popular round length, but you can do a slightly shorter or longer round if appropriate. In our quizzes, we often do a round that combines history and maths. For example:

What do you get if you multiply the number of Apollo missions that landed on the moon by the number of people who've walked on the moon, then add the year that this first happened.

$(11 \times 12) + 1{,}969 = 2{,}101$

It's quite good fun, but if the sums are more complicated it can take a while, so you wouldn't want to do more than five of them. Picture rounds, on the other hand, can be a bit longer. You generally leave your contestants to work these out as a team, so a selection of 20 famous faces or unwrapped chocolate bars to identify gives them plenty to get their teeth into.

If you're doing a less formal quiz at home, then you can really have fun playing around with different ideas for rounds and games. Some will be more successful than others, but if you're really lucky you might hit on a winning format that becomes a family or friend-group favourite. Who knows, you might even come up with something so brilliant that you sell it to a TV company, it becomes an international smash hit, and you get to come and talk about it on *Fingers on Buzzers*!

# FORMATS TO TRY

## Purist

### Last One Standing

A classic spin on *Fifteen to One*. Fire questions at your contestants one by one; when they run out of lives they sit down. Only one can win! A simple format, which works in big groups or small – especially useful when there are an uneven number of players to divide into teams.

### Interrogation

Recreate the intensity of *Mastermind* by sitting your players down in a solitary chair in the middle of the room before firing questions at them against the clock. Increase the intensity by turning all the lights off except one lamp pointed directly at them. Raise the tension further – the room is pitch black, and everyone is wearing head torches and staring at the quizzer.

You could even add in a specialist subject round, if you have time to prepare beforehand. Otherwise, you might keep it ultra-specialist, quizzing the contestant on the other members of the party, family members or even objects in the room.

### Beat the Smughead

Pay tribute to the civilian vs professional formats such as *Eggheads* and *The Chase* by selecting your own 'Smughead' i.e. the best quizzer in your group. Can the rest of you team up to overpower them on general knowledge? Can the Smughead even be dethroned and replaced in a bloodless quiz coup?

(Smugheads is what my nana calls the *Eggheads*.)

**LUCY SAYS:**
We missed out on *Eggheads* glory because one of my teammates (naming no names but he's a *Homes Under the Hammer* presenter whose name rhymes with Bartin Boberts) couldn't identify Alexander McQueen's bumster trousers.

## Gimmick

### *Keep Calm and Quiz On*

A genius quiz show gimmick of the early noughties was *The Chair*, hosted by John McEnroe. Contestants could win big, but only if they kept their cool and their heart rate stayed low. It seemed very high-tech at the time, but these days you can use a basic fitness tracker or even the pulse detector on an exercise bike which is gathering a light layer of dust in the corner.

### *Roll On, Roll Off*

Never underestimate the addition of a physical skill element to liven up a quiz. One of our favourites of recent years was the short-lived BBC daytime quiz *The Edge*, which was sort of a delicate bowling contest. Players would roll a ball along a flat platform with different prize zones marked on it; the closer to the far end the ball stopped, the bigger the reward . . . as long as it didn't fall off altogether. Clear off the kitchen or coffee table for this one, and use any sort of light ball. Or you can roll coins (if you still have any in the cashless society). The more questions you get right, the more chances you get to roll.

### The Golden Shot

Actually, no. Please leave this to the professionals (Bob Monkhouse et al.). Crossbows aren't lawful.

---

**QUIZ – GENERAL KNOWLEDGE**

Here's some good old-fashioned general knowledge quizzing for you all!:

1. Which English monarch was the uncle of the late Queen Elizabeth II?

2. Who invented a reading system for the blind in the 1820s?

3. Name two of the four presidents' faces carved into Mount Rushmore.

4. Which was the first country to give women the vote in 1893?

5. What do you get if you cross a raspberry with a blackberry?

---

6. What was first opened to the public in Montagu House, Great Russell Street in 1759?

7. David Myers and Simon King are better known by what name?

8. Which sea lies between the coasts of Italy and Croatia?

9. What is the collective noun for geese on the ground?

10. What did Francis Crick and James Watson first discover/clarify in 1953?

11. Who wrote *The Unbearable Lightness of Being*?

12. Which is the only one of the Seven Wonders of the Ancient World still in existence?

13. Who wrote the lyrics to *Jesus Christ Superstar*?

14. Who survived a shooting in 2004, only to be shot in September 2006 in Las Vegas?

15. What is the name of Tony Soprano's wife?

16. Who was stripped of his 100 metres gold medal at the 1988 Olympics after failing a drugs test?

17. Janet Leigh was memorably killed in the shower at the Bates Motel in 1960. What was the name of her character in the film?

18. Who was the first explorer to reach the South Pole?

19. London Zoo is situated at the edge of which London park?

20. What was the name of the policeman in *'Allo 'Allo!* who spoke terrible French?

# THE
# GENERATION
# GAMES

2

## DERMOT FINCH ON *BLOCKBUSTERS*:

Dermot was a contestant who managed not to answer a single question correctly on *Blockbusters*.

*'I think the producers thought we were doing it on purpose . . . We were sent by our headmaster to win a minibus. We came back with £40 and a dictionary . . . I started at Liverpool University the week that was shown on telly. So I was in Fresher's week at Liverpool University and total strangers were coming up to me going, "I've seen you somewhere before." One bloke came up to me and said, "You made a right idiot of yourself!" It was my 15 minutes of humiliation . . . but now it's a celebration.'*

One of the joys of quiz is that it's a hobby that can be enjoyed by young and old alike.

For many families, Christmas or other holidays are the times we all get together to play games. In this situation, the best kind of quiz is one where people of all ages can take part and have fun. This is tricky to achieve.

You have to make sure that the references are gettable for everyone – if several generations are competing, and you ask a question starting 'Which famous Harry . . .', contestants may immediately start thinking about Harry Potter, Harry Styles or Harry Secombe, depending on their age. See also Olivia Rodrigo / Olivia Newton-John and Taylor Swift / Shaw Taylor.

**LUCY SAYS:**

For young people, taking part in quizzing can be a quick way to acquire new knowledge and satisfy their curiosity about the world. As an older person, quizzing does all the same things, plus it can also give useful reassurance that your faculties are still somewhat intact. I've just entered my fifties and I can't always remember where I left my glasses, why I came into the room or the names of my husband and children, but I can remember every single word to 'It's Raining Men' by The Weather Girls.

TV quiz and game shows are generally open to everyone over the age of 18, with no upper limit. Questions are generally designed to be as broad in their appeal as possible.

There have been some games and quizzes that have made a feature of the fact that team members or competitors come from different generations – obviously there's *The Generation Game* and *Ask the Family*. In recent years people enjoyed being challenged with *Are You Smarter Than a 10 Year Old?*

**LUCY SAYS:**

*Are You Smarter Than a Ten Year Old?* is all very well, but there appears to be a gap in the market at the other end of the spectrum. Should we have a quiz where the young pit their wits against older people? We could call it *Are You Smarter Than My Nan?* In my nan's case, she knew how to get a GI to give her a pair of silk stockings and how to shoplift a frozen turkey from any branch of Bejam. Would today's youth be able to match that?

The schedules have always been full of programmes for specific groups of younger people. When I was growing up there was *Top of the Form* for schoolkids, or the more anarchic *Runaround* and *Cheggers Plays Pop. University Challenge* predominantly features people in their late teens and early twenties, with the odd mature student. *Blockbusters* went for an even more niche category – sixth-formers. So let's take a deeper look at that show.

# BLOCKBUSTERS
## Fact File

**NAME:** *Blockbusters*

**DATES:** First run from 1983 to 1993, with various reboots since

**CONCEPT:** Sixth-formers try to make their way across a board of hexagons. They are given the first letters of the answer to general knowledge questions and have to guess the rest. There's one team of two players, pitted against a maverick solo player.

**HOSTS:** Bob Holness in the first instance, with Michael Aspel, Liza Tarbuck, Simon Mayo and Dara Ó Briain keeping the flame alive subsequently.

**PRIZES:** Various wholesome items designed to keep the teenagers out of trouble: dictionaries, cardigans, even a Filofax! (Ask your parents.)

**FAMOUS WRONG ANSWERS:** There was the unfortunate contestant who said 'orgasm' when they meant 'organism', but our favourite was:
'What "L" do you make in the dark when you're taking a wild guess?'
The answer should be 'Leap', but the contestant said 'Love'. They had a point.

## BLOCKBUSTERS

This legendary quiz was based on an American format of the same name, and initially ran from 1983 to 1993 on ITV. It's been rebooted in various forms in later years.

There were three contestants on each show. Debate rages in quiz circles about the fairness or otherwise of having a solo player pitted against a team of two. We personally think it was a genius move, as it gave it a David vs Goliath feel. You always rooted for the solo player as the underdog, but there was often one person on the duo team who was dead weight, and watching the furious glares of the superior player as their companion gave a dumb-ass answer was priceless.

Whereas the US show had been a quiz for adults, the beauty of the UK version was that the competitors were sixth-formers – adorable nerds between the ages of roughly 16 and 18. This is probably the age where you're at your most self-conscious and awkward, and when you almost certainly shouldn't expose yourself to the glare of publicity.

And kids of the 1980s were definitely not the social media savvy teenagers we see nowadays. As an adolescent in the 1980s, there were two main ways to interact with television sets: become a ram-raider and smash a Ford Mondeo into the window of Dixons, or appear on *Blockbusters*.

Our host was the avuncular Bob Holness. A kindly, twinkly man who was falsely (and bafflingly) accused of (or credited with, depending on how you feel about it) playing the saxophone solo on Gerry Rafferty's hit single 'Baker Street'.

The beauty of *Blockbusters* was its clear visual gameplay – boards made up of hexagonal tiles that the contestants had to navigate their way across to win. Each hexagon contained the initial letter of the answer (or multiple letters in the later 'Gold Run' round). Contestants would request a letter and then be given a question. For example: 'Which D is a popular current TV show about the oil industry set in Texas?'*

*Dallas

This caused much hilarity when the contestants said, 'Can I have a P please, Bob?' because it sounded like they wanted to do a wee. Towards the end of the show's run, as rave culture took hold, the request 'Can I have an E please, Bob?' suggested they were asking for drugs.

Speaking of rave culture, we can't leave the subject of *Blockbusters* without mentioning the hand jive. On Fridays, AND ONLY ON FRIDAYS, the contestants would be allowed to do a little upper body workout along to the theme tune. At the time we adored this. If the show was made now, presumably there would be full-blown TikTok dances every day, with twerking, dabbing, slut drops etc. Gosh, the 1980s was a more innocent time.

It's also worth mentioning the prizes. If you did really well on *Blockbusters* you might win some money, but the main prize was a sweatshirt or a cardigan. Also, because this all happened in the 1980s, they occasionally gave away a Filofax!

Just to complete the 1980sness of it all, computer game

versions of the show were created for the Commodore 64 and ZX Spectrum.

## WHAT CAN WE USE FOR OUR OWN QUIZZES?

Giving a letter as the hint to an answer. You could even do a round where all the first letters spell something out. For example:

**QUIZ – *BLOCKBUSTERS***

1. What S do Americans call a student who is in their second year at university?

2. A is the country with Mount Kosciuszko as its highest mountain?

3. What N is the country containing Fiordland National Park?

4. What T is an everyday word that has mixed Latin and Greek roots, meaning 'far sight'?

5. What A had a bandleader named Glenn Ponder on his ill-fated chat show?

6. What C is the particular interest of a cruciverbalist?

7. What L is a metallic element and a track on Nirvana's album *Nevermind*?

8. What A is an English football team who play their home matches at the Crown Ground?

9. What U was created when a hippo took an apricot, a guava and a mango, and then the python picked the passion fruit, and the marmoset the mandarin?

10. What S is an HBO TV show starring Jeremy Strong and Sarah Snook?

# ASK THE FAMILY
## Fact File

**NAME:** *Ask the Family*

**DATES:** 1967 to 1984 with Robert Robinson; 1999 with Alan Titchmarsh; 2005 with Dick and Dom

**CONCEPT:** Two families face questions, riddles, music and picture rounds.

**HOSTS:** See above. Also, Dave Chapman, who played comedy characters in the 2005 series like *Mastermind*'s John Humphrys and Robert Robinson, was a quiz show host who also presented Radio 4's *Today* programme. Green-fingered Titchmarsh hosted a revival on UK Gold before Dick and Dom brought it back to the BBC.

**PRIZES:** No prizes AT ALL for the weekly winners – what a swizz. There was the prize of a family PC for the series winners. People weren't keen on the Dick and Dom revival but at least on every episode the families received a decorated plate to reward them for turning up.

**SAMPLE ROUND:** BIRDS

Which bird appeared on the farthing from 1937 to 1956?

Wren

A pen is the female of which bird?

Swan

Which birds fed Elijah in the desert?

Ravens

Which bird is known poetically as *philomel*?

Nightingale

Which bird was the symbol of Athens?

Owl

**BRAIN TEASER:** The twins Jane and June each had a £10 note so that they could buy their own birthday present. Jane spent twice as much as June, and June received three times as much change as Jane. How much did they each spend on their present?

## ASK THE FAMILY

This show ran from 1967 to 1984 with host Robert Robinson, and it has been rebooted with Alan Titchmarsh and Dick and Dom at the helm.

There were two teams of four players – usually a mum and dad and their two teenage children.

The original version was much derided because it generally featured only terribly 'naice', middle-class, nuclear families. Endearing dweebs basically. (*Not the Nine O'Clock News* parodied it with a sketch where all the contestants were quantity surveyors, including the children.)

The stand-out element was a picture round, where teams had to identify a familiar household object from an unusual angle. This is a really easy one to do at home, especially now we all have camera phones with zoom lenses, and it's even better than the TV show because you can use it to poke fun at each other: 'Oooh! That's the toenail clipping that dad left on the bathroom sink.'

## RUNAROUND
## Fact File

**NAME:** *Runaround*

**DATES:** 1975 to 1981 with Mike 'Frank Butcher' Reid. Various other hosts filled in for Mike or hosted spin-offs and reboots, including Johnny Vegas in 2002.

**CONCEPT:** General knowledge quiz for children which involved, well, running around.

**HOST:** Mike Reid. Not, it has to be said, a natural children's TV presenter. A veteran stand-up comic, he addressed the children like they were a particularly rowdy stag night.

He'd call the children 'wallies' when they got an answer wrong. Probably wouldn't get away with it today, but great fun to watch.

**PRIZES:** A lovely snapshot of bygone days, the kids could choose from stuff like:

- Pocket camera with flash
- Fountain pen and pencil set
- A pair of wildlife books
- An amazing stereo radio cassette machine

The show winner got to choose their prize first, then the other children descended on the prize table like hyenas feasting on a gazelle.

**CATCHPHRASE:** You think you know? Well g-g-gooooo-oooooooooooo!

**STAND-OUT MOMENTS:** When the contestants are introduced at the top of the show, their hobbies are read out. Like the prize selection, this really takes you back. Practically all of them are model railway enthusiasts or stamp collectors. Our other favourite element of the show is when they take a break from the quizzing to do an educational bit. Sometimes they'd have a potter demonstrating how to throw pots on a wheel, or a falconry display. The hundreds of hyped-up kids in the studio had to suddenly calm down and concentrate. Admittedly, they managed this better than Mike Reid, who looked absolutely bored stiff.

## RUNAROUND

It was hosted by comedian and actor Mike Reid – better known in later years as Frank Butcher in *EastEnders* – and was again based on a successful US format.

Groups of kids were asked a general knowledge question with three potential answers, and they had to run to a specific area marked one, two or three to signify their choice. Just before the answer was revealed, Mike would shout 'Run around now!', giving the players the chance to quickly shift answers and confuse their opponents. Everyone who stood in the right spot would get a coloured ball to put into a tube. At the end of the game, the player with the fullest tube would win.

The best moments in the show were when one maverick child would stick to their chosen answer in the face of everyone else deserting them – and be proved right. There was often chaos as the kids tried to trick each other by standing on the wrong answer until the last possible second.

If you're organising a quiz outdoors (especially with energetic children), it can be great fun to replicate the gameplay, by making your contestants run around the garden. You could even do it indoors, as long as you don't mind vases and lamps going flying when players make a last-moment dash to the right answer. This is an evergreen, if exhausting format – we even played a version on a cruise ship recently, and it's as fun and tense as ever. Especially with adults who have been on a drinks package.

**LUCY SAYS:**

Inter-generational quizzing is great, but sometimes you do want to compete against people your own age and ask age-specific questions. For my 50th birthday, my old friend Mel set a quiz for me and my mates that was entirely about bands of the 1990s. We had great fun with it, but it would have been baffling for anyone who didn't know their Oasis from their Elbow.

**OUR FAVOURITE . . .**

### SAUCY MOMENTS IN QUIZZES

Kids, put down the book right now – this part is just for the grown-ups. We're going to take a moment to talk about the saucy bloopers on TV shows.

Obviously everyone remembers Bradley Walsh on *The Chase* being reduced to fits of giggles by the name of German skier Fanny Chmelar, but some other questions and puzzles have provoked similar reactions.

### *EGGHEADS*

The question was:

'Which world leader was pictured topless, fishing in a river in Siberia in 2007 and again in 2009 riding a horse?'

The options were:
Angela Merkel, Kim Jong II or Vladimir Putin
Confronted with the mental image of a bare-chested Angela Merkel, Jeremy Vine completely lost it!

## COUNTDOWN

So many rude words have come out on the letters round, but our favourites, just for the studio reactions, were: wanker, slutz and bumhole. Seeing Susie Dent having to repeat 'bumhole' is up there with my wedding day and the births of my children as a happy memory.

## CATCHPHRASE

There's a legendary episode where the bonus catchphrase – the one where an image is gradually revealed by removing squares – seemed to feature cheeky mascot Mr Chips, erm, pleasuring himself. The winning phrase turned out to be 'snake charmer', but it was only revealed after much hilarity in the studio. Roy Walker kept it all together brilliantly, but then he couldn't hear the obscene suggestions that were being shouted out in houses up and down the country.

## BLANKETY BLANK

Of course, the questions in *Blankety Blank* are often designed to elicit saucy answers, but the brilliant comedian Roisin Conaty managed to get in a sexual innuendo that nobody saw coming! The question was 'Gregg Wallace's bald head looks so much like an egg that when I see it I want to BLANK it'. Everyone else went with smash, crack or boil. Seems a bit violent, but Gregg does elicit strong reactions. Clearly Roisin has feelings about him, because her answer was 'lay'.

## FAMILY FORTUNES

*Family Fortunes* is where most of the really saucy moments happen. Again, the writers know exactly what they're doing with some of the questions. If you ask, 'Name somewhere you wouldn't expect to meet a nun.' Who wouldn't blurt out 'brothel'? When they asked, 'Name something apart from a door that you open,' they must have known they were inviting both 'legs' and 'bowels'!

Sometimes even seemingly innocent questions can provoke weird answers, though. Here's our list of some very strange *Family Fortunes* answers – see if you can match them to the questions:

| | |
|---|---|
| Name something you wouldn't try even once | Just a small prick |
| Name something the dentist says | Sex |
| Name something everyone has more than two of on their body | Wheels |
| Name something that comes in sevens | Naomi Campbell |
| Name a bird with a long neck | Red Riding hood |
| Name something a car has more than 2 of | Fingers |
| Name something accociated with The Three Bears | Sex on a train |
| Name something your partner can't manage without | Legs |
| Name something you close | The Tin Man |
| Name something associated with Alice in Wonderland | Arms |

## QUIZZES – OLDER PEOPLE and YOUNGER PEOPLE

Since this chapter is about the joy of quizzing for all, we've included a set of questions for the older members of the family, as well as another set for the younger ones. You can decide yourself which age bracket you fall into.

So we'll start with a question requiring five answers, then count down to a question that needs only one answer:

## QUESTIONS FOR THE OLDER PEOPLE:

### QUESTION ONE – pick one of the below (you have to write down five things):

a. Name five of the eight Ivy League universities.

OR

b. Name the five US states with a Pacific coastline.

OR

c. Name five of the eight British prime ministers since 1900 with the shortest surnames i.e. they all have five letters or fewer.

### QUESTION TWO (you have to write down four things):

a. Name four of the five landlocked countries in the EU.

OR

b. Name the four years in the 20th century in which the king or queen of the United Kingdom died.

FINGERS ON BUZZERS

**QUESTION THREE (you have to write down three things):**

a. Carnivore or Herbivore:

a) Stegosaurus b) Komodo dragon c) Duck-billed platypus

OR

b. Apostrophe or not. Do the following brand names have an apostrophe in them when correctly written out (all according to the company websites)?

a) Morrisons b) McDonalds c) Halfords

**QUESTION FOUR (you have to write down two things):**

a. Guess the years:

a) Jacques Chirac becomes president of France, Nick Leeson is arrested for his role in the collapse of Barings Bank, and OJ Simpson is found not guilty of the murders of Nicole Brown and Ronald Goldman [who had been killed the previous year].

b) *Starlight Express* opens at the Apollo Victoria in London, the first MTV Music Awards are held in New York, the UK and China agree to return Hong Kong to China in 1997, and Scarlett Johansson is born.

OR

b. Mystery years:

a) Terry Waite is taken hostage, *The Herald of Free Enterprise* capsized, and Kylie Minogue releases 'The Locomotion'.

b) The computer 'Deep Blue' wins at chess against Garry Kasparov, Charles and Diana are officially divorced, Dolly the Sheep is born, and François Mitterrand dies.

**QUESTION FIVE (you only have to write down one thing):** What links the number 'five' in Spanish, 'four' in English, 'four' in German, and 'three' in Italian?

## QUESTIONS FOR THE YOUNGER PEOPLE:

**QUESTION ONE (you have to write down five things):**
a. Name five of the eight primary planets in our solar system.

OR
b. Name five of the seven continents of the world.

**QUESTION TWO (you have to write down four things):**
a. Name the four capital cities of the United Kingdom.

OR
b. Name the four cardinal points of the compass

**QUESTION THREE (you have to write down three things):**

a. Are these characters from the Marvel universe or the *Star Wars* universe?

a) Luke Skywalker b) Black Widow c) Thanos

OR

b. Are these US states or UK counties?

a) Kent b) Vermont c) Tyrone

**QUESTION FOUR (you have to write down two things):**

a. Guess the scientist:

a) She was born in Poland in 1867, discovered polonium and radium, and was the first woman to win a Nobel Prize.

b) He went on a five-year trip on the HMS *Beagle*, has a research station on the Galapagos Islands named after him, and best known for his theory of evolution.

OR

b. Name the pop star:

a) She was born in the USA in 1989, has won 11 Grammy Awards, and her songs include 'Shake It Off', 'We Are Never Ever Getting Back Together' and 'Look What You Made Me Do'.

b) He was born in England in 1994, he was in the band One Direction, and his songs include 'As It Was' and 'Watermelon Sugar'.

**QUESTION FIVE (you only have to write down one thing):**

The German word for 'no' sounds like which number in English?

# ON YOUR BUZZERS

## MARK 'THE BEAST' LABBETT, CHASER
## ON *THE CHASE*:

*'At the beginning of* The Chase *they told us not to be mean, they told us to just do the facts. But me being me, I started being a little bit playful, a bit of sledging and stuff, and the focus groups picked up that actually they kind of liked it; it was just playful abuse. If I'd just called someone "You're a stupid beeping idiot", obviously they wouldn't be very happy, but if you make a thing, going "oh dear, oh dear, oh dear". . . Effectively, all the tools I had as a teacher, slapping down the kid verbally, I did it on the contestants. Effectively, my whole life has been job training for this.'*

We called our podcast *Fingers on Buzzers* because it's such a commonly used phrase in TV quizzes. It's evocative and almost Pavlovian – how many coffee tables and sofa arms are used as unconscious makeshift buzzer buttons while watching *University Challenge*?

The year 1948 is accepted as the first TV outing of the thrillingly modern electric buzzer, on the American show *Winner Take All*. One player had a buzzer, the other had to make do with an old-fashioned bell. You'd be annoyed, wouldn't you?

Since then, we've become very accustomed to hearing some kind of jarring electronic noise during our quiz shows. And these buzzers and sound effects can be used to signify all kinds of things: a contestant wants to answer a question; they've got the answer right; they've got the answer wrong; it's the end of the round or show. There's even the legendary 'Golden Buzzer' on *Britain's Got Talent*, which brings its own chaos, joy and confetti.

These days, buzzer systems and sound effects are utterly high-tech and programmed to be ultra-sensitive – after all, they need to work out to the millisecond who buzzed first, and block any other contestants from buzzing in late.

**OUR FAVOURITE . . .**
QUIZ SHOW BUZZERS/SOUND EFFECTS
*University Challenge* buzz-ins with the legendary Roger Tilling announcing the contestant's name and university/college. Unlike on other shows where this is pre-recorded, Roger actually reads this live in the studio – which explains why he seems to get faster and more animated as the episode nears its end.

The *Family Fortunes* wrong answer sound. Literally sounds like a computer saying 'uh oh!' – we all recognise this as the sound of failure.

Eranu and Uvavu from *Shooting Stars*. Eranu for a right answer, Uvavu for a wrong answer, and instead of a hooter to denote the end of the quiz, the scorekeeper (usually George

Dawes or Angelos Epithemiou) would come up with a wacky alternative noise. Vic and Bob even created custom buzzer sounds for their panellists, which was unique at the time. *Shooting Stars* was an innovative and irreverent reworking of the traditional panel show. Ostensibly chaotic and silly, it was interesting to see how much of the traditional structure they kept – team captains, a scoring system, the same rounds every week . . . clearly there are some things you can't do without.

LES DENNIS APPEARING ON *THE CHASE*:

*'I did well in the cash builder but I got convinced by Joel Dommett to go for the £80,000 and I was doing OK until a question came up about twerking and I had no idea what it was, so I went out.'*

## THE CHASE
## Fact File

**NAME:** *The Chase*

**DATES:** 2009 to present

**CONCEPT:** A team of quizzers face off against some of the world's best (and most attractive) quizzers.

**HOST:** Bradley Walsh (plus six – absolutely stunning – Chasers)

**PRIZES:** Largest sum ever won by a team is £100,000. Largest individual win is £80,000.

**CATCHPHRASES:**
'It's time to face the chasers'
'For you, the chase is over'

**QUESTIONS THAT HAVE REDUCED BRADLEY TO HELPLESS LAUGHTER:**
What 1993 film was concerned with activities around Gobbler's Knob?
*Groundhog Day*
Dump, floater and wipe are terms used in which team sport?
Volleyball
In what sport does Fanny Chmelar compete for Germany?
Skiing

## THE CHASE

### The Quick-Fire Round

A thrilling part of many TV quizzes is the 'quick-fire round'. Often on a TV or radio show this is used as the final round. The contestants have to buzz in to answer the questions first, and sometimes the round is given a fixed length to increase the tension.

There's a reason the quick-fire round at the end of a show is so popular. By firing a lot of short questions at contestants and allowing the one who buzzes in fastest to answer, you can drastically alter the scores they've accumulated in the earlier rounds. It means that there's everything to play for right up to the last minute.

The quintessential example of this is the final chase on *The Chase*. Let's take a look at why this works so well by examining the shape of the show.

## The Cash Builder

There's an urgency to this first round because it's against the clock, which gets the show going at a cracking pace. We also get a sense of how good the contestant's general knowledge is, and how quick their reflexes are.

## The Head-To-Head

Then the players are up against the Chaser on multiple choice questions, and the speed of the show relaxes slightly. We get to see Bradley Walsh have fun with the contestants and trade witty insults with the Chaser. This is where you get the classic moments like Bradley losing his mind over the name of German skier Fanny Chmelar. This is where we get to know the personalities of the players.

The most controversial element of *The Chase* is probably the negotiation with the Chaser. The contestant can either compete for the amount of money they accumulated in the Cash Builder, try to win more money by accepting the Chaser's higher offer, or make things easier for themselves by taking the low offer. Viewers take to social media enraged when the lower offer is taken, but quite often that is tactically the right thing to do.

## The Final Chase

Then things become all swift, businesslike and tense. The remaining contestants go first, and get two minutes to buzz in and amass as many points as possible, before the Chaser gets their two minutes to try and surpass the team's score. By now, we have an idea about the team's strengths and weaknesses, and we are rooting for them to win (speak for yourself – J). There have been some thrilling final chases.

**LUCY SAYS:**

I've been lucky enough to appear twice on *The Chase*, winning once and losing once. The final chase is so tense. You don't want to buzz in too early with a wrong guess, but you don't want to waste valuable time waiting if none of you knows the answer. Also, although it goes quickly on TV, two minutes is actually quite a long time to concentrate on quick-fire questions. If you're ever appearing on the show, it's worth doing some training for that round specifically.

**JENNY SAYS:**

Regular viewers of *The Chase* already know that the magic threshold for a team's score is 20. Any score they set for the Chaser which begins with a two gives them a stonking chance of success – backstage, the Chasers will term this a 'free go' because the contestants have done a great job and all we can do is hope to get on a good run to even get close to them.

Unfortunately for them, this means we relax a bit and play more freely. My favourite ever Final Chase was in 2017. On seeing the team I immediately recognised Charlie, the player in seat four, as a threat – I'd seen him playing for Manchester on a recent series of *University Challenge* – and I was proved correct when he chose the high offer and sailed back with £84,000. Meaning I was playing a full house for £100,000. In the final he was even more valuable to the team by answering 15 questions correctly, a rare feat. I faced a total of 24, which is considered almost unbeatable.

Almost.

I relaxed, and somehow caught them with 14 seconds left. Uncharacteristically, the one question I got wrong was about gin (yes, we hard-core quizzers still remember the ones we get wrong for years!)

Of course I felt for the team – they had every right to think the money was going home with them, with such a great score. And especially I felt for Charlie. The experience hasn't put him off, though – he's still quizzing, and I am sure he's plotting his revenge . . .

# *ONLY CONNECT*
# Fact File

**NAME:** *Only Connect*

**DATES:** 2008 to present

**CONCEPT:** The quiz show lover's quiz show. Hard questions presented as entertaining puzzles to two teams of brainiacs.

**HOST:** Victoria Coren Mitchell

**PRIZE:** Just a trophy, but really, appearing on the show itself is the prize.

**NOTABLE CONTESTANTS:** Jenny Ryan!!! (and Mark Labbett) plus many of the UK's finest quizzers.

## HOST WITH THE MOST: Victoria Coren Mitchell

We adore *Only Connect*, and a large part of its appeal is Victoria's sense of fun and enthusiasm. She's not afraid to put on a silly costume if that's what it takes to serve a punchline. She's clearly very clever, but she wears it lightly. She's often visibly delighted by the questions, and respects the art of the question setters. The contestants clearly love her, and she loves them right back. What could be a very dry, intellectual quiz is leavened by Victoria's mischievousness. She's also become the absolute number one pin-up for dads who listen to 6 Music.

JENNY HAWKER, AN *ONLY CONNECT* PRODUCER
ON VICTORIA COREN MITCHELL:

*'She's made it into a little world. It could just be a really straightforward, difficult quiz, and I think it would still work as that and I think people would still really enjoy playing it. But she makes it so playful and she's sort of in on the joke. I love that she can laugh with and at the contestants. I just think that's so fun.'*

We talk at various points in this book about the difficulty of definitions – what makes a quiz show different from a game show or a panel show etc. But let's take a moment here to celebrate the 'puzzle' show. We'll deal in depth elsewhere with shows that wrangle with words, numbers and pictures.

## *PUZZLING*
## Fact File

**NAME:** *Puzzling*

**DATES:** 2023 to, er, 2023 when this book was written

**CONCEPT:** Memory tests, mental arithmetic, puzzles and wordplay are all used in this format. It's a veritable cornucopia of quiz. Six players are randomly divided into two teams, until the final round where the winning team revert to being individual players.

**HOST:** Lucy Worsley, beloved historian and presenter, with a very impressive title in her day job: Chief Curator of Historic Royal Palaces.

**OUR FAVOURITE ROUNDS:** *Puzzling* has revived the 'memory test' aspect of game shows that we so enjoyed in classics like *The Krypton Factor*.

In the 'Memory Bank' round, the contestants are shown a board with 15 words on it, and they have to remember the placing of those words. Then the words are replaced with their numbers, the players are asked questions and have to construct the answers by naming the numbers that conceal the correct words.

So, if word 8 was 'California' and word 3 was 'Hotel', and the question was 'What was the title of an Eagles hit single?', the contestant has to answer '3, 8', but if the question was 'What was the name of a Mamas and the Papas hit single?', the contestant would have to remember that 'Dreaming' was the word hidden behind square 12 and answer '8, 12' for 'California Dreaming'.

The 'marmite' section in this quiz is the 'Pressure Points' round, which combines mental arithmetic with observational skills. The teams are shown a picture, they then have to count the number of things in that picture, and then perform a mathematical operation on those things. For example, there might be a number of red flowers in the picture on the left, and a number of yellow flowers in the picture on the right, and contestants have to multiply the red flowers by the yellow flowers.

## *PUZZLING*

This new rival to *Countdown* has recently launched on Channel 5. Although in the cosy world of sit-down puzzle shows, I'm not sure that the term 'rival' is really appropriate.

We've only seen the first series so far, but the wonderful mixture of general knowledge, wordplay, maths and memory make for great fun and are perfect to incorporate into your at home quiz.

In the show the 'Pressure Point' round is done against the clock by one player at a time, but we thought that for your home quiz it might make a good buzz-in round. You can keep the maths element quite simple, and make the hard bit counting up the things in the pictures. That way you're giving an advantage to the younger players with their quick little brains.

Here is an example: Oranges minus apples equals what?

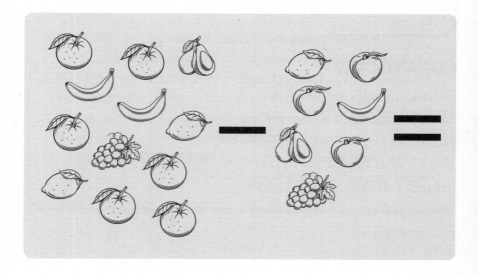

## COUNTDOWN Fact File

**NAME:** *Countdown*

**DATES:** 1982 to present day, making it one of the longest-running TV quiz shows

**HOSTS:** Richard Whiteley (1982–2005), Des Lynam (2005–2006), Des O'Connor (2007–2008), Jeff Stelling (2009–2011), Nick Hewer (2012–2021), Anne Robinson (2021–2022), Colin Murray (2022–present). However on this show the co-hosts are equally important, notable mentions include Carol Vorderman (1982–2008), Susie Dent (1992–present), Rachel Riley (2009–present).

**CONCEPT:** Contestants compete against the clock as they undertake a series of word and number tasks.

## COUNTDOWN

Solving puzzles or riddles against the clock has been done in many ways on TV. Sometimes you have to stand up while you're doing it, and maybe run about a bit (*The Cube*, *The Crystal Maze*) but sometimes you're allowed simply to sit behind a desk.

*Countdown* is hands down the grand champ of the sit-down puzzling shows. Everybody knows that it launched Channel 4 in 1982, and Richard Whiteley soon became everyone's favourite cheesy uncle. Then it was hosted with varying degrees of success by some newcomers, until it was delivered into the safe hands of Colin Murray in 2022.

The show is based on an original French format, 'Des chiffres et des lettres' (thanks to my 324-day streak on Duolingo I know this means 'figures' and 'letters').

There are only three elements to the gameplay:

1. Teasing the longest word possible out of a random selection of nine letters
2. Making a randomly generated three-digit number out of six smaller numbers
3. Unscrambling a 'conundrum'. A perfect nine-letter anagram.

As we constantly say, when coming up with a format, simplicity is your friend. The fact that everyone on the show is very familiar with the rules allows the producers to add other fun elements to spice things up a bit. There's Susie Dent helping out with defining the words, and increasing our love of the English language a little bit more every day. There's Rachel Riley showing us how to do the sums. There's a celebrity guest telling stories, making up poems or just being Gyles Brandreth – he's the most popular of the dictionary corner residents, with over 300 appearances. That's a lot of novelty jumpers!

*Countdown* is such a winning formula that it's even become a wildly successful night-time comedy panel show, in partnership with *8 Out of 10 Cats*.

The contestants on *Countdown* are allowed to come back up to eight times, when they become Octochamps! Which must be the coolest thing ever.

---

## *FAMILY FORTUNES*
## Fact File

**NAME:** *Family Fortunes*
Based on the American *Family Feud* (with many spin-offs and variations, see below)

**DATES:** 1980 to present day, with a few gaps

**HOSTS:** Bob Monkhouse, Max Bygraves, Les Dennis, Andy Collins, Vernon Kay and Gino D'Acampo

**PRIZE:** Cash, cash, cash, plus a car or holiday for the winners and some spot prizes

**CONCEPT:** Families battle other families to work out how other people think.

---

## *FAMILY FORTUNES*

Legend has it that Bob Monkhouse himself rejected the American title *Family Feud* because he thought it sounded too aggressive. His decision has been resolutely vindicated. *Family Fortunes* is one of the cosiest and cuddliest shows on the telly.

The format is another triumph of simplicity. A family –

captained by its mouthiest member – plays off against another, and they have to name things in categories, trying to guess which of those things will be the most popular. They win cash corresponding to the number of people (out of 100) who gave that answer, so it's in their interest to gauge the national mood carefully.

It's kind of a reverse *Pointless* if you will.

At the end of the show, the family that's scored the most points gets to nominate two members to answer five questions against the clock.

It's fascinating to watch an early episode side by side with a contemporary one. The format may have remained the same, but everything else has changed.

The set these days is a big showbiz affair with glittering city lights. In the early days the set featured an answer board so lo-fi it made Ceefax look like 8K UHD. The contestants also exude more confidence – some of the early participants look like they're in a hostage situation rather than a TV game show. Of course, the make-up of the families has changed. Max Bygraves raised an eyebrow when he had to introduce an unmarried couple who LIVE TOGETHER! but now there are many more blended families, step-parents and same-sex couples. Even when they ask the same questions over the series, you get very different answers in different eras.

I've seen the question 'Name something you might do on a first date' answered with 'go to a roller disco' in the 1980s and 'book a hotel room' in the 2020s.

### HOST WITH THE MOST: Les Dennis

All the hosts have had their charms. Slick Bob and Cuddly Max set the show up, but they handed it on to a host who was slick, cuddly and absolutely delightful. Les was known to all as a comic and impressionist, but he was a game show natural (plus he did manage to smuggle that incredible Mavis Riley impression into the show every now and then). The winning contestants regularly swept Les off his feet in their excitement at the end, so evident was their affection for him.

Les joined *Family Fortunes* in 1987 in the wake of a huge personal tragedy. He told us:

'When I went into *Family Fortunes*, I'd been in a double act with Dustin Gee, and Dustin died on 3 January 1986. People said, "What is Les going to do?" I'd lost my comedy partner, and I'd lost this extraordinary career that was happening for both of us. My agent at the time said, "They want you to consider *Family Fortunes*," and I remember thinking, "No, I can't do that. I won't be any good at it," because I hadn't worked with the public in that sense. I learned on the job and luckily they let me do that. In that first series we did 26 shows in four weeks. Having watched particularly Bob I thought, "I am going to have a joke for every contestant." And that's what I did for the first few shows, before I realised I should let it come organically. That's Bob style and I was trying to emulate someone else's style.'

Les is regularly asked about his favourite of the legendary wrong answers from the show, but he told us about a lesser known one, involving one of his *Family Fortunes* predecessors:

'The question was name something associated with Dracula –

you'd think bats, teeth, coffin, stake. He went, "Bob Monkhouse!" No idea to this day what he was thinking.'

LES DENNIS, HOST OF *FAMILY FORTUNES*:

*'Who were the hundred people in "We asked a hundred people"? The contestants! The people that were coming in for the series, we would give them the questions for the next series. That's why we got so many silly answers.'*

If you want to include a quick-fire round in your home quiz, you might need to improvise a bit . . .

**JENNY SAYS:**

We can't all have a sophisticated system of buzzers that can work out to the millisecond which contestant was fastest. I mean, I do, of course, but most homes don't have the luxury.

## BUZZING AT HOME

Here are some things to bear in mind:

## Needle in a Haystack

Giving your opposing players buzzers with distinct sounds will make the quiz master's job much easier. If everyone is buzzing by tapping their glass, then it will be impossible to work out who is first. Also you'll probably have broken glass, red wine stains and tinnitus to deal with by the end of the night.

## Not All Buzzers are Equal

Players using an electronic buzzer might have a quicker reaction time than someone who has to, say, pick up and shake a maraca. This isn't always a bad thing – you can use it as a handicap system to temper your stronger quizzers and give others a chance.

## Noise Control

Perhaps just have one buzzer per team. Signed, your neighbours.

## Top Tip

Raid the games cupboard and the charity shop! There are loads of board games (not just quiz-related ones) that have a buzzer in the box. Or there are plenty of things around the gaff that will do the job.

We've tested out a few things we found around the house and rated their usefulness as a buzzer:

*Bee in a cup* – 1/10. Impractical, and also we should be protecting bees not forcing them to work for us.

*Wasp in a cup* – 0/10. Hazardous, although this may happen

anyway if you're having a garden party quiz with sugary beverages.

*Medic alert button* – 0/10. It will test some reactions, but Nan will be furious.

*Whatever instrument the kids are learning at school* – 9/10. Bound to be attention-grabbing and shrill.

*Doorbell* – 2/10. Classic button-pressing format but you won't be able to hear the questions properly from the doorstep.

*Torch* – 8/10. Excellent for deaf quizzers – but the QM will need an assistant to keep an eagle eye out.

The most lo-fi solution is just getting your contestants to shout out their name, or any word or noise. You can be quite strict with this. If someone shouts out the answer without first remembering to honk, squeak or sing the opening bars of Beethoven's fifth, feel free to deny them a point. The number one rule of quizzing is that you have to follow the rules!

## QUIZ – COUNTDOWN

The final round of *Countdown* – the famous '*Countdown* Conundrum' can be fiendishly tricky. The premise is that they've mixed up a nine-letter word and you need to unscramble it.

We've come up with a list of our favourite nine-letter-word anagrams, plus we've written a little *Countdown*-style clue that might help you guess it.

For example:

On *Countdown*, you might choose a 'snotcanon' (Consonant)

OR

The most musical animal is the 'carthorse' (Orchestra)

Here are some more to solve:

1. If you're feeling sluggish, you might need some 'lightcare'?
2. I decided to say 'I do' because of a 'heartbolt'
3. I find it objectionable when a 'malehoots'
4. A cry in the dark from a 'dingogoth'
5. You're very bold when you 'meshseals'
6. I have a traffic stopping 'blackdoor'
7. This branch of science might give you a 'moralclue'
8. Are you getting rid of that 'Shoebasil'?
9. First thing in the morning you should 'bakefarts'
10. This diplomatic HQ needs 'cleanouts'

Of course, you can come up with these yourselves. You could use an online anagram generator, or just an old-fashioned pen and paper and your brain.

**2**

NAME ..................

SCORE ..................

**1**

NAME ..................

SCORE ..................

**3**

NAME ..................

SCORE ..................

4

# A QUESTION OF SPORT

TREVOR BROWNING, CONTESTANT ON *BULLSEYE*:
Trevor was the non darts player – the 'knower' not the thrower. Between him and his partner, Des, they had to get 101 in six darts. Trevor scored treble 20 with his first dart, and with his second dart . . . treble 20! Des never even had to step up to the oche.

*'Before we went on we said if we're lucky enough to get to that stage we'll just gamble. It's a once in a lifetime opportunity!'*

*'We won a Talbot Samba – the pinnacle of British engineering! We were given the option that night – we could either take a cash equivalent which was about £1,750, or they would get us a Talbot Samba sorted out and insured and we could drive it back the next day, or we could wait until August and get the new plate which would make it easier to sell. We opted to do that, got it delivered to the local Talbot dealer in Aldershot and he sold it for £3,000, so we got £1,500 each.'*

Sports rounds are hard to get right in quizzes. Some people love sport and have a wealth of facts and figures at their fingertips (Jenny), but other people shudder at the mere mention of balls, and believe that Tiger Woods was where the 'Winnie the Pooh' books were set (Lucy).

At any pub quiz, the announcement 'The next round is . . . sport' can be met by an equal number of cheers and boos.

So, how do you set questions that are challenging enough for football aficionados, but also interesting to people whose idea of a physical challenge is seeing how many Jaffa cakes they can fit into their mouth at once?

Let's take inspiration from some of our favourite TV shows. Sporting quiz and game show formats have been enduringly popular on British television, but there's one programme that's seen off all-comers, and remains the champion of champions:

## *A QUESTION OF SPORT* Fact File

**NAME:** *A Question of Sport* (then *Question of Sport*) (It had a different title – *A Question of Sport* – until 2021. No one knows why they dropped the 'A'. Maybe the BBC needed it for a new programme?)

**DATES:** 1968 onwards

**CONCEPT:** A show for sportspeople, by sportspeople, with sportspeople, about sportspeople

**HOSTS:** David Coleman, David Vine, Sue Barker and Paddy McGuinness

> **PRIZE:** They're sportspeople, they don't need a trophy, they just live to WIN!

## A QUESTION OF SPORT

A *Question of Sport* (or latterly *Question of Sport* – don't know what prompted the name change) celebrated its 50th anniversary in 2020. There was a pilot episode in 1968, but the show proper began in 1970, and has been hosted by the two Davids – Vine and Coleman – Sue Barker and Paddy McGuinness. Its list of team captains and guests is an absolute Who's Who of British sporting legends. Even HRH Princess Anne has guested on the show.

*AQOS* mixes picture rounds, general sporting knowledge and specific rounds on particular sports. There's a pleasant sense of jolliness and mayhem. The mystery guest round is a particular highlight. This is where a famous sports star is filmed from unusual angles and/or wearing a cunning disguise. The funniest moments are where it's someone who's mega famous or a close personal friend of someone on the show and still nobody guesses correctly.

The format was so successful that various other spin-offs were tried including *A Question of Pop*, *A Question of TV*, *A Question of Entertainment*, *A Question of Scotland* and the more niche *A Question of EastEnders*. None of these enjoyed the longevity of the original. Granada's Men and Motors channel even made

*A Question of Sex*, which was clearly nothing to do with *AQOS*, and rest assured that Sue Barker had nothing to do with it!

Sports stars seemingly love appearing on it, because it lets them prove that they've got mental acuity to match their physical prowess. They're given the option to answer questions on their own field of excellence or sports in general, so everybody gets a chance to shine.

The secret of its success is that it's fun even if you aren't that into sport.

**LUCY SAYS:**

I discovered *A Question of Sport* in the 1980s, when it was hosted by David Coleman, and team captains included cheeky Scouser Emlyn Hughes (Scousers are always 'cheeky', we don't make the rules) and cuddly Bill Beaumont.

Thinking about it, Bill Beaumont's cuddliness might have been a factor in my sexual awakening (note: might want to discuss this with my therapist rather than in print). My dad was a huge fan of rugby union and an Arsenal fan. I didn't care for rugby or football, but I could play along anyway. My favourite rounds were 'Sports Star from a Mystery Angle' and 'What Happened Next?' I cottoned on quickly that what happened next was usually an animal invading the pitch, or a footballer scoring a spectacularly stupid own goal.

★ ★ ★ ★ ★ ★ ★ ★ ★ ★ ★ ★ ★ ★ ★ ★ ★ ★

**FUN FACT: HRH Princess Anne appeared in 1987 – making her, as far as we know, the only member of the royal family to appear on a TV quiz show. Although I bet Queen Camilla fancies a go on *Tipping Point* – we can put you in touch, Your Majesty.**

★ ★ ★ ★ ★ ★ ★ ★ ★ ★ ★ ★ ★ ★ ★ ★ ★ ★

### 🎤 HOST WITH THE MOST: Sue Barker

We must give a special mention to Sue Barker, who crowned a very respectable tennis career by becoming one of the first female quiz hosts, with an impressively long tenure, from 1997 to 2021.

## OUR FAVOURITE . . .

THEME TUNES

Somewhat ironically, musicians and composers are the unsung heroes of TV. The right theme song can ensure that a show lives on in the public's memory, even when the final credits have rolled for the last time. Here are ten of our faves in no particular order:

### GOING FOR GOLD

There's probably a no more beloved theme tune in the history of daytime TV. Surely everyone knows by now that this catchy tune was composed by Oscar-winning film composer Hans Zimmer. Yes, the epic soundtracks to *Gladiator*, *The Last Samurai* and *Dunkirk* are fine, but for our money, this is his greatest work. Its cheeriness perfectly matched the upbeat joy of everyone's favourite Euro quiz.

### THE CHASE

Paul Farrer is one of the UK's most eminent TV composers, and can count *The Wheel*, *Gladiators* and *The Weakest Link* among his many successes. Obviously we have a special affection for *The Chase* theme tune. Lucy's children say that one of their earliest memories was of hearing that 'rang, dang, diddly, diddly' just before they got their tea. Very much like Pavlov's dogs, they still perk up every time they hear it, sensing that fish fingers may be imminent.

### THE CRYSTAL MAZE

Zack Laurence was responsible for this one, as well as the theme for another Channel 4 smash, *Treasure Hunt*. What we love about it is that it's so epic and scary. The genius of *The Crystal Maze* is how anxious it makes you feel about the fact that someone might get locked in the room if they fail to complete the puzzle. Their fellow contestants, along with the viewers at home, are screaming 'GET OUT NOW!!!' despite the fact that they're in NO physical danger WHATSOEVER. This theme song really captures that sense of panic and impending doom. It's the soundtrack for the end of the world.

### POINTLESS

Marc Sylvan is another titan of TV show theme writing. Like all the greats, he has a distinctive style, yet manages to make every track he writes feel fresh and relevant to the show. His quiz show credits include *Tipping Point* and *The Million Pound Drop*, but we love this jaunty piece, with its tooty horns that you can sing along to.

### COUNTDOWN

We have so much love for Alan Hawkshaw. A legend in so many ways, he came up with so many certified bangers, including the Channel 4 news theme. We all know that *Countdown* was the first show broadcast on Channel 4 in 1982, so Alan's theme tune was right there at the start of the new channel. Carol Vorderman claimed in her autobiography that Alan composed it on the toilet. Next time you're answering nature's call, why not give yourself a countdown at the end and finish off with that 'bada, bada, badalada!' flourish? Alan used his royalties from *Countdown* to offer scholarships to new musicians, so he was a thoroughly decent man, as well as a musical god.

### MASTERMIND

A piece by Neil Richardson called 'Approaching Menace', this tune is appropriately regal for a show that crowns the kings and queens of quizzing. It does also have the appropriate air of, well, menace that the black chair creates. Richardson also co-wrote the very sprightly tune 'Scotch Broth' which accompanied the 'little girl and terrifying clown' test card on the BBC between 1969 and 1972.

## WHO WANTS TO BE A MILLIONAIRE?

Keith Strachan co-wrote Cliff Richard's Christmas smash 'Mistletoe and Wine', which would probably be enough of a lifetime achievement for most people. Not for Keith though, he also (with his son Matthew) composed the music for what is probably British telly's most successful worldwide export. Viewers the world over have thrilled to the tension beds which ramp up the suspense, the little flourishes that accompany right and wrong answers, and the theme itself. It's dramatic – it needed to signal that a large amount of money is at stake, but it's got the thing that every theme tune should have: even though there is no official singing, the words of the title fit to the tune, so that you at home can belt out 'WHO WANTS TO BE A MILLIONAAAAAAAAIRE?' at the end.

## ASK THE FAMILY

*Ask the Family* was regularly derided for its middle-class conformity, but for much of its life it had the most groovy, trippy theme tune on TV. The track was called 'Acka Raga' by Indian composer John Mayer and Jamaican-born saxophonist Joe Harriott. Mayer was an orchestral violinist who played with the Royal and London Philharmonics, but he also had an experimental Indo-Jazz fusion project on the side. They were commissioned to write this tune, with Mayer on sitar. It's a swirly delight, and one of the few quiz show themes you could stick on at a student house party without harshing the vibe.

### GIVE US A CLUE

Originally this ITV parlour game used Alan Hawkshaw's tune 'Chicken Man', which you'll probably know better as the theme tune to BBC's *Grange Hill*. A later version of the theme, composed by Alan Braden, is the one we love though.

It features classic cheesy session singers like so many theme tunes (*Blankety Blank*, *Supermarket Sweep*) but it gave them a lot more to do. In this theme song, they not only explained the rules of the game, they even sang the presenter and team captains' names.

If you're having a game of charades at home you could sing this at the start! Look it up online for the tune and the excellent lyrics.

### LIGHTNING

We loved Zoe Lyons' show *Lightning*, and the soundtrack was one of the best we've heard in ages. It's another Marc Sylvan creation, and perfectly in keeping with the futuristic look of the titles and set. When Zoe was on our podcast she had this to say:

'I love the set and I love the theme tune because it's a bit *Tron*-esque. And the lasers in the set are brilliant. Then it turned out that Will, the lighting director is, like me, a bit of an old raver. He's been to a lot of clubs in the nineties and I said, "This is where it's come from . . . Ministry of Sound."'

## FURTHER AFIELD

*A Question of Sport* may have dominated the field, but British TV has hosted numerous other sports quizzes, including:

At the vanguard of the 'laddish' culture of the 1990s and early 2000s, *They Think It's All Over* featured some legendary banter and memorable rounds. Chief among these was 'Feel the Sportsman', where popular athletic figures of the day were subjected to very intimate examinations by the blindfolded panellists who simply had to guess their identity. This is definitely one we wouldn't recommend playing at home!

*Play to the Whistle* is a more recent show that caters to the casual sports fan by featuring physical challenges rather than endless facts and stats. Similarly *A League of Their Own* provides more comedy banter. This show will go down in history as the place where Mo Farah invented the Mo-bot celebration!

As well as these general sports quizzes and game shows, there have been plenty of TV hours dedicated to specific sports. *Big Break* brought snooker tricks to the masses thanks to John Virgo, while *Tarby's Full Swing* put golf in the spotlight.

## *BIG BREAK* Fact File

**NAME:** *Big Break*

**DATES:** 1991 to 2002

**CONCEPT:** Pro snooker players pot balls, members of the public answer questions. Trick shots are played for a bit of light relief.

**HOST:** Jim Davidson

**FORMAT:** This format must surely have owed a debt to mega-hit *Bullseye*, and the BBC cast a stand-up comic with a cheeky charm, matched with someone from the sport in question. In this case, the very laid-back, sardonic John Virgo.

**PRIZES:** A *Bullseye*-style mixture of cash and prizes. Modern tech like microwave ovens and fridge-freezers, with a mystery star prize. A consolation prize was a very snazzy John Virgo waistcoat.

**THEME SONG:** 'The Snooker Song', written by Mike Batt for his musical *The Hunting of the Snark*, featuring the famous line, 'I'm gonna be snookering you tonight.' The theme was sung by Captain Sensible – former member of punk band The Damned, and a vegetarian anarchist and pacifist. He probably wouldn't have seen eye to eye with host Davidson on many things.

**ODD FACT:** There's a weird Mandela effect, where a lot of people seem to remember the theme song being Chas and Dave's 'Snooker Loopy'.

**UNEXPECTED SCENE STEALER:** *Big Break* attracted all the megastars of snooker, which was huge on TV at the time. A big difference between *Big Break* and *Bullseye* was that the members of the public were paired with professional snooker players. This added great entertainment value, as some pro players acquitted themselves admirably, and some struggled. Stephen Hendry, Willie Thorne and other household names all featured, but it was always a treat when the show featured

Dennis Taylor with his big glasses, and his surprising flair for delivering jokes like: 'I was feeling a bit nervous backstage, so I had a little Scotch and Windolene out the back there. I feel a bit tipsy but my eyes are as clear as a bell!'

*Bullseye* is one of the most enduringly popular shows, and probably the one which our listeners mention most often in their all-time top three. We're devoting space to it in almost every chapter of this book, which is testament to its genius. *Bullseye* introduced an entire generation to the steely nerves, unflinching aim and surprisingly quick grasp of maths that's required when throwing the arrows.

## BULLSEYE Fact File

**NAME:** *Bullseye*

**DATES:** 1981 to 1995, then one series in 2006

**CONCEPT:** Teams of two – a 'knower' and a 'thrower' – answer questions and throw darts to win cash and prizes.

**HOSTS:** Jim Bowen 1981 to 1995, Dave Spikey 2006

**PRIZES:** Cash (counted by hand by Jim and presented in a silver tankard) and prizes from the legendary prize wall.

**CATCHPHRASES:**
'You can't beat a bit of bully'
'Super, smashing, great'
'Let's have a look at what you could've won'
'Keep out of the black and in the red – there's nothing in this game for two in a bed'

**LUCY SAYS:**

I've never had much interest in sport, but back in 1997 I worked on a show called *What's the Score?* It was a quiz for children about football. It went out on ITV in the Granada region, and it was hosted by the lovely Brendan Coogan. I helped write the links and research the questions, so I do know a bit about sport, but only very specifically about football in the North West of England in the late 1990s. At pub quizzes my teammates will be astonished when – having sat mute throughout an entire sports round – I suddenly leap in with the answer to:

In 1998, Stan Ternent followed England star Chris Waddle as the manager of which club? (Burnley FC)

**JENNY SAYS:**

Most of my sport quizzing happens on the Radio 5 comedy panel show *Fighting Talk*. While – technically – the questions we face don't have a 'correct' answer, there's a lot of fun to be had thinking up opinions and researching weird and wonderful facts from the world of sport in an effort to impress the judge (who assigns points – and deducts them – on a whim). This subjective type of game is pretty good as an off-the-cuff entertainment over dinner or down the pub, as it combines a bit of knowledge with debating ability and – crucially – knowing what will impress the person in charge. During Colin Murray's tenure as host, I knew that any references to Liverpool FC I could drop in would boost my score, but I really needed to avoid cricket chat if I wanted to win. You can, of course, expand the game to any topic and debate at length: Who is the best Belgian? When does 'middle age' begin? Where sells the best pasty? (The last one is extremely contentious in my home town of Bolton.)

## QUIZ – SPORT

Test the strength and depth of your sporting knowledge with the following 20 questions:

1. Prix de l'Arc de Triomphe is awarded in which sport?

2. Which sportswear company was founded by Adolf Dassler in 1924?

3. Which two sports comprise a biathlon?

4. In which sport could you encounter the terms 'yuko', 'koka', 'ippon' and 'waza-ari'?

5. In which sport is the Webb Ellis Cup awarded?

6. 'Shakehand' and 'penhold' are the two most common types of grip in which sport?

7. In which sport did Duncan Goodhew represent Great Britain?

8. In US sports, what is the name of the NFL team from Cleveland?

9. The phrase 'up to scratch' originated in which sport?

10. In which sport are the Miller and Rudolf moves performed?

11. An early version of which sport was known as 'poona', before it took the name of a house in Gloucestershire?

12. Which sport is the subject of the film *Cool Runnings*?

13. In 1984, the BBC Sports Personality of the Year Award was given to two people. Who were they?

14. In which athletics event could you see a Western roll or an Eastern cut-off?

15. Orenthal James are the first names of which infamous American sportsman?

16. David Wilkie and Mark Spitz achieved fame in which sport?

17. The Stanley Cup is a famous trophy in which sport?

18. Which sport is played according to the Cartwright rules?

19. Which sport involves a sheet, stones and a brush/broom?

20. Which sport is played on the larger field, cricket or polo?

5

SCREEN TEST

When you reach the half-time point of a pub quiz, it's traditional for the picture quiz to make its appearance.

While you're getting a round in, queueing for the ladies or phoning home to make sure the kids haven't driven the babysitter mad, everyone can have a look at the sheet of pictures and venture a guess.

Let's take a long hard look at the picture round.

In a pub quiz you can just leave a sheet on the table and let the contestants work it out in their own time. Or you can make it a round in the body of the quiz if you have some kind of projector and/or screen at your disposal. There's even the potential to set rounds involving film clips relatively easily.

We've all got a lot more used to video elements in quizzes these days, or indeed doing whole quizzes in our homes thanks to Zoom, Teams or other video calling platforms. Some of us have become experts at hosting virtual quizzes thanks to our experiences in lockdown.

(Just a quick note for anyone who's picked up this book far in the future, by 'lockdown' we are referring to the Covid-19 pandemic which confined us to our homes for much of 2020 – and beyond. Unable to go out and socialise, a lot of us turned to quizzing for comfort. At first, this was just people reading out questions on video calls, but as the months wore on, people became more technically savvy and learned how to share their screens so picture rounds and even video rounds were possible.)

**LUCY SAYS:**

It's no exaggeration to say that quizzing saved my sanity in lockdown. I am a naturally very sociable person (I know that sounds like a euphemism for 'drunk') and really missed seeing friends and especially going to our regular pub quiz.

My friends very quickly got online quizzes up and running, and I loved it. Sometimes I would take part in two or three in a week and I never got sick of it. It was good to have something to look forward to after a day of doing Joe Wicks workouts, baking sourdough loaves and attempting to home-school the kids.

Some great new formats for rounds came out of this time – we'll be sharing some of these with you further on. There was still space for the classic no-frills general knowledge quiz though. I'd like to give a special shout out to Keith Severs, whose alphabet quiz was both a social highlight and a very demanding mental workout.

# *CATCHPHRASE*
## Fact File

**NAME:** *Catchphrase*

**DATES:** 1986 to 2002, then 2012 to present

**CONCEPT:** Say what you see! Identify popular phrases, represented as pictures, and win prizes.

**HOSTS:** Roy Walker and Stephen Mulhern have stuck at it longest, with mini stints from Nick Weir and Mark Curry in the middle.

**PRIZES:** Cash and some other prizes. The 'Super Catchphrase' jackpot of £50,000 was first won in 2016.

**CATCHPHRASES:**
'Say what you see!'
'It's good, but it's not right'
'Will the middle solve the riddle?'

## *CATCHPHRASE*

*Catchphrase* is another programme which straddles the worlds of quiz show and game show, but it's definitely tipping over to the game show side of the fence. The general knowledge element is really just being au fait with common English phrases or titles of things.

Youngsters might find this hard to believe, but at its inception in 1986, the graphic wizardry of *Catchphrase* was breathtaking. We'd been used to seeing *Blue Peter* features on how long it took to make a single frame of animation and how it involved hundreds of people. So imagine our awe when cartoon host Mr Chips skidded on to our screen with his brightly coloured moving illustrations. I was so impressed I almost dropped my Angel Delight.

Essentially Mr Chips was a 2D Dusty Bin. A mute co-host for Roy Walker to play some gags off, and to keep the show rolling along.

What we have always loved about this show is when people repeat the wrong answer to themselves again and again, trying to get it to make sense. Once your brain has decided that the phrase you're looking for is 'Man with a bird!' it's hard to convince yourself that it's actually 'A bird in the hand'. It's fascinating to see someone else's brain caught in a loop, unable to move on.

The celebrity version of *Catchphrase* is a lot of fun, because in the standard version if someone doesn't know the answer, the game tends to move on before they can get TOO embarrassed. On *Celebrity Catchphrase*, Stephen can drag things out for as long as he likes and leave Jenny Powell trying to guess 'Pride comes before a fall' but she's just stuck repeating the word 'Pride, pride, pride' endlessly, like she's an old-time preacher haranguing a sinner.

# WHAT CAN WE USE FOR OUR OWN QUIZZES?

If you've got any keen young artists in the family, it can be fun to let them show off their artistic skills by creating some *Catchphrase*-style visuals ahead of time. Either a picture or, if they're particularly tech savvy, a short animation. Even if it does mean that the kids then realise how many really creepy phrases there are in the English language: 'spill your guts', 'makes your blood boil', and 'over my dead body' are all ones that our young relatives particularly enjoy.

If you do want to include a visual element in your quiz, here are some ideas. Potential picture rounds include:

## Celebrities

The simplest premise, but a classic. It's just a photo of a famous face, and you simply have to provide their name. These rounds can be surprisingly hard. As we have discussed elsewhere, anything involving celebrities depends on the age and frame of reference of your contestants.

Sometimes you can give this a twist by making all the celebrities sportspeople or politicians. Or you can add a fun theme, like they were all born on the day that you're holding the quiz.

Another popular take is to use photos of celebrities as babies, children or teens. Given that all babies look like Winston Churchill or Ken Bruce that's a good guess to go for if you're not sure. There are many American high school yearbook photos available online. Jerry Seinfeld is a bit of a classic. If it's a baby photo from the Victorian era and it looks like a girl

112

it's probably a boy and vice versa. It's actually a refreshing change from the current fad for dressing girl babies like Disney princesses and boys in onesies saying 'I'm a boob man, like my dad'. We live in weird times.

Sometimes with picture rounds it's a nice touch to give a little clue. For example we were given a photo that turned out to be Adele as a baby, with the clue: 'Rolling in the diapers'.

Another theme you can use is awards which link the famous faces – the more unlikely, the better. When *Fingers on Buzzers* went 'on tour' and did a live show in Guernsey, we did a picture quiz in honour of our guest Anneka Rice, on the theme of 'Rear of the Year' winners (Anneka won in 1986 alongside Michael Barrymore). Getting the correct answer by glimpsing the rear alone must be worth at least double points. Other unusual awards include Celebrity Mum of the Year, Glasses Wearer of the Year and Pipe Smoker of the Year. (This finished in 2014 and was never won by a woman! There are glass ceilings left for us to smash.)

## Movie posters

There are some iconic images out there – think how many people would recognise the posters for *Pulp Fiction* or *The Shining*, even if they've never seen the movies. You can opt for either small details from posters or the whole thing. My friend Toby did a brilliant round of African movie posters, where the artist had drawn their impression of the movie – clearly sometimes without seeing it.

## Album covers

Same deal as movie posters. If you're a whizz with Photoshop it's good fun to replace the faces in photos with pictures of your friends and family. For my friend Jo's birthday we did an online quiz and featured a round of album covers from the 1990s with her face on all of them.

## Close-ups of things

Another classic. We loved it as a round on 1970s/80s favourite *Ask the Family*. It's great if you can use things from around your own home to personalise this. For a quiz at my children's school we took photos of parts of the classrooms and playgrounds and they loved the challenge.

## Logos

Those clever little graphic designs are everywhere, but sometimes it's hard to recall whether you've seen that little squiggle on a pair of trainers or a packet of washing powder. As well as general brand logos you can go more specific with airline tail logos, vehicle logos, alcohol brands etc. You can use local shop signs to make it a bit more personal if you're quizzing with friends and neighbours.

## Emoji-based questions

Everyone loves emojis right? 🎬 *Richard Osman's House of Games* brought this to our screens with the round 'Totes Emoji'. You can use emojis to convey the titles of films (*The Emoji*

*Movie* is a good place to start) or song titles. Emoji Tube stations is a round I've participated in, which is fun if a bit London-centric.

### Road signs

Combine quizzing with a little bit of brushing up on your Highway Code. My fave is 'no cars or motorcycles' which looks like an Evel Knievel stunt.

### Geography-based pictures

The world really is your oyster here, as you can choose from: Flags / maps / shapes of countries / landmarks / city skylines in silhouette etc.

### Works of art

An excuse to look at some beautiful paintings, photographs or sculptures. You can simply ask contestants to name the artist, or if you're dealing with connoisseurs you might demand that they give the title of the piece as well, or even the art movement from which it derives.

### Food

It's tricky but fun to identify unwrapped chocolate bars, individual biscuits, chocolate selection boxes without the lid or – for the savoury fan – pastry-based items from Greggs.

## Fashion
Identify the designer of these outfits, shoes, handbags . . .

## Other consumer items
Toys we have loved
Unusual fruits and vegetables
Pasta shapes (ask for the names in Italian)

## What Happens Next?
Now that it's relatively easy to incorporate images or video clips into a quiz, why not make your own PowerPoint or keynote presentation and include some surprising moments of your own? These could be the sporting disasters familiar from *A Question of Sport*, or you could use YouTube clips of skateboarders falling over or surfers wiping out. If you've got any home videos that feature dad hurting himself while trying to jump into the pool on holiday, or Auntie Sally falling off a child's trike, they can add a personal touch to proceedings.

## Sports star from a mystery angle
You can do your own photo round featuring cropped pictures of sporting stars or legendary moments. Here's one to get you started:

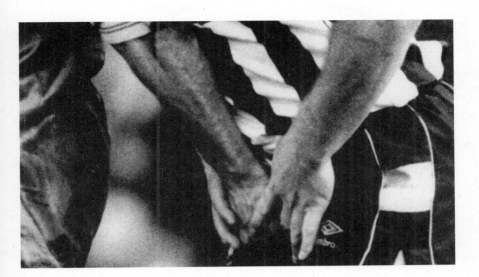

Which hard man actor is grabbing another footballer by the soft bits here?

BONUS POINT: Name the other player.

POPMASTERS

**LUCY SAYS:**

May I just take a moment to say something controversial? I hate music rounds in pub quizzes.

This may come as a surprise to *Fingers on Buzzers* listeners, who will know that I am a massive fan of 'PopMaster' (my feelings about Ken Bruce are well documented). I grew up on *Name That Tune*, screamed with delight when Duran Duran were on Mike Read's *Pop Quiz* and I enjoyed being a panellist on *Never Mind the Buzzcocks* in the early 2000s. Nonetheless, when the quiz host at my local presses play on their laptop, I'm often tempted to head to the bar.

The music round is a staple of quiz. However, it can be quite a frustrating part of the night. The essential problem with it is that there are very few variations in format. You get played a clip of a song then have to give the title and/or name the artist. Alternatively, you might just hear some lyrics read out and have to identify which song they come from.

The frustration arises because essentially, after a couple of bars or lines, you either know it or you don't. And you have to be quiet. It's the enemy of the essential joy of a pub quiz: having a row with your teammates.

If the round is just questions about music, that's fine – then you can have all the fun of finding clues in the question and arguing about what the answer might be.

For example, you might be asked: 'Which Sheffield-based band, fronted by Glenn Gregory, had a hit in 1983 with

"Temptation"?' Immediately, Sheffield in 1983 gives us three main options: ABC, The Human League and Heaven 17. Then you might rule out The Human League because you know the lead singer was Phil Oakey. But then there's room for debate, discussion (finding the name Martin Fry, but still being unsure whether he was from ABC or Heaven 17) and singing the song quite badly at each other in the hope that it might help.

Whereas if I just hear a clip of the song, or the lyrics: 'I've never been closer, I tried to understand, that certain feeling carved by another's hand', there's nothing but my own imperfect memory to help me out. (That is an excellent lyric by the way – kudos to Ian Marsh / Martyn Ware / Glenn Gregory.)

For quiz setters I understand the temptation (sorry, that word, and the song, are now lodged in my head) of a music round with audio clips. For a start, it breaks up the monotony of hearing the quizmaster/mistress's voice.

Plus, the execution of the music round has become so much simpler in recent times with the advent of digital technology and the internet. I remember going to quizzes in the 1990s where the quizmaster would have to use a clunky CD player and change the CD for each track, running the risk of the disc skipping or of accidentally playing more of the song than they'd intended. Then, if a team wanted a question repeated, they'd have to fumble around to find the right CD and try to remember which bit they'd played. Now it's relatively easy to edit together a little package of clips and repeat it as often as you like.

Nonetheless, I still find something slightly unsatisfying about the whole business. The quiz I go to most regularly has a slightly more (ahem) mature clientele, so they're on pretty safe ground if they use music clips from the 1970s to the 1990s, but we are all flummoxed if something more modern comes up. There's nothing more depressing than seeing blank faces and shrugging shoulders. They're the true signs of quizzers who have given up hope.

Interestingly, music quizzes on TV have had a somewhat chequered history, particularly in the UK. Radio has had a much more successful relationship with them – the aforementioned 'PopMaster' and Radio 4's more classically skewed *Counterpoint* with Paul Gambaccini are long-running successes.

On telly, *Name That Tune* is the big daddy. The US version has run in various forms on and off from 1952. Its current incarnation boasts Jane Krakowski as host (whom I have loved from *Ally McBeal* and *30 Rock*) and *American Idol* judge Randy Jackson as musical maestro.

In the UK it started in the 1950s as *Spot the Tune*. The retitled and revamped *Name That Tune* was a ratings winner in the 1970s and 1980s, hosted by game and quiz show legends Tom

O'Connor and Lionel Blair. There was also a revival fronted by Jools Holland for Channel 5 in the 1990s.

The beauty of this format is that it circumvents the main problem for music quizzes on TV – getting permission or 'clearance' to use the original songs.

You might wonder why there aren't more music-based quiz shows – or indeed, movie or TV-themed series – with plenty of clips. And the reason may be the mysterious 'clearance'.

In essence, broadcasters need to be covered by a licence if they want to use recorded music, film or TV clips – this is so the creators end up with the correct credit and payment (eventually, anyway!)

Bigger broadcasters have wide-ranging licences which cover thousands of pieces of music – but still not every piece of music can be used, and permission can even be withdrawn by the creator – so every single bar must be 'cleared' legally. As you can imagine, this isn't a straightforward or cheap process, and lots of producers would rather avoid jumping through so many hoops just for a few seconds of a song!

There is an exception for what is called 'fair use' – that is, when a clip is used in an editorial context, such as on the news or on a review show. *Jukebox Jury*, therefore, was able to play lengthy clips as the songs were being reviewed by the panel!

Essentially, *Name That Tune* uses its in-house musicians to provide cover versions of songs, which also gives it the excitement of a live performance.

Another genius part of the format is 'Bid a Note'. This is

where contestants compete to identify a song from the tiniest fragments. They can offer to guess the tune from any number of notes between one and seven.

One player might say, 'I'll name that tune in six,' but if their opponent is cavalier enough, they might offer to do it in three or four. If they succeed they win the point, but if they don't have enough notes to go on, the other player gets to hear all seven. In a recent US show that I saw, the most daring player bid five, and the first five notes of 'Barbie Girl' by Aqua were all it took to secure victory – after all, five notes is all it takes to get the memorable hook 'I'm a Barbie Girl . . .' and no accompanying vocals were required.

## *NEVER MIND THE BUZZCOCKS* Fact File

**NAME:** *Never Mind the Buzzcocks*
(For younger readers, it's a play on the name of the Sex Pistols album, *Never Mind the Bollocks* and the popular punk/new wave band Buzzcocks.)

**DATES:** On and off since 1996 on BBC2, it's been on Sky since 2021.

**CONCEPT:** Panel show with pop stars and comedians being rude to each other and to older rockers.

> **HOSTS:** Mark Lamarr, Simon Amstell, Rhod Gilbert and Greg Davies, plus all the great and the good of UK showbiz as guest hosts. Noel Fielding has been a perennial favourite as team captain, and Daisy May Cooper and Jamali Maddix are excellent new additions for the Sky series.
>
> **PRIZE:** It's a panel show, so just bragging rights.

## NEVER MIND THE BUZZCOCKS

In the UK, our most successful TV pop quiz of recent years has been *Never Mind the Buzzcocks*. It started in the heyday of laddishness – 1996 – helmed by Mark Lamarr. From 2006 until 2014 it was mostly under the control of guest hosts, with longer stays from Simon Amstell and Rhod Gilbert. Recently it was rebooted on Sky Max in 2021 with Greg Davies. Team captains have included Phill Jupitus, Sean Hughes, Bill Bailey, Noel Fielding, Jamali Maddix and Daisy May Cooper.

The most memorable elements of *Buzzcocks* have been:

- 'Guess the Intro' – this is where contestants have to render all the instruments vocally, with varying degrees of success.
- 'Identity Parade' – a round that largely served as a vehicle to humiliate old pop stars and one hit wonders.
- 'Next Lines' – essentially a classic complete the lyrics round, made funny by the fact that pop stars often failed

to recognise the words from songs they'd written or recorded.

*Buzzcocks* has had its controversial moments – most notably with guests storming off the show or being visibly disgruntled by the teasing or outright cruelty of the hosts. Lemmy from Motorhead, Huey Morgan and, most famously, Preston from the Ordinary Boys have all expressed their displeasure.

One major factor which makes a successful music-based quiz is playalongability; this usually involves singing or shouting answers at the telly and annoying the neighbours. This was quite successfully done in the Shane Richie series *Don't Forget the Lyrics*, which was a quiz by way of karaoke – big money could be won by singing the correct words to a song. This was particularly brutal when the line you needed to fill in was from the obscure third verse rather than the chorus.

More recently (and even more annoyingly for my neighbours) has been the BBC's *The Hit List*, which is essentially an exercise in identifying songs at speed from clips. For some reason the function of the buzzer switches between rounds – sometimes it's to interrupt with an answer, sometimes it's to skip the track, and this is anxiety-inducing but compelling.

# POP QUIZ
## Fact File

**NAME:** *Pop Quiz*

**DATES:** 1981 to 1984 plus other specials over the years, most recently for BBC4 in 2016/17. In the 1980s, the show got 10 million viewers every week.

**CONCEPT:** Pop stars face off on their specialist subject – pop music.

**HOST:** Mike Read and Chris Tarrant (one series in 1994)

**PRIZE:** The honour of being Top of the Pops (at quizzing)

## MIKE READ, HOST OF *POP QUIZ*:

'We got people that you didn't get on panel games, like members of Queen, Led Zeppelin, George Michael, Morrissey . . . you didn't get Morrissey on panel games. It was a show that people wanted to be on and still do! . . . The real rowdy ones of course were Duran (Duran) and Spandau (Ballet) which was a real big ratings show. I think it was a really difficult one for the team to edit because every time someone smiled, scratched their ear, blew their nose, the audience went *crazy! It was an absolute nightmare for the bloke with the razor blade. And they were at each other right from the start – Duran always reckoned that Spandau cheated.'*

We also asked Mike, which pop star would you have on your pub quiz team?

*'I would go for Paul Young – Paul is very good – or Nick Heyward'*

## POP QUIZ

A great example of the TV pop show genre, one that we'd love to see resurrected: *Pop Quiz* with Mike Read.

*Pop Quiz* originally ran between 1981 and 1984, hosted by Radio 1 stalwart Mike Read (not Mike Reid, he was *Runaround* – see the chapter on Generation Games).

The beauty of the format was that the contestants were all pop stars. Very occasionally you'd get a DJ like John Peel; bafflingly, Little and Large were once allowed on. But mostly just actual pop stars with songs in the charts. It was like a weird spin-off from *Top of the Pops*. Team captains and contestants included Toyah, Roger Taylor, Phil Lynott, Hazel O'Connor, Meat Loaf, and (my favourite) Green from Scritti Politti.

The quiz itself was very straightforward – they just played clips of songs and questions were asked. They couldn't get rights to the videos presumably, so they'd just play them over old silent films or animations. Or occasionally a proper video of a performance that the BBC owned like *Top of the Pops*. It was rather like a musical *A Question of Sport*; they had the same 'mystery guest' feature (although with a bonus clue – a song playing backwards accompanied the clip), and a 'Guess the Year' round. Other rounds included mashed-up songs, identifying lyrics and cover versions.

It was utterly joyful to any music fan at the time to see, for instance, George Michael rubbing shoulders with Rick Wakeman or Dave Edmunds. There was a particularly memorable episode which pitched Spandau Ballet against Duran Duran – there was, understandably, hysteria and chaos in the studio audience.

A distillation of the early 1980s, *Pop Quiz* was always a great watch. From the theme tune – a frenetic synth track with people shouting and whispering the words *Pop Quiz* – to the big shiny set, to Mike Read's baffling array of looks (ranging from a mullet to a Purdy cut) to the hysterical studio audience, screaming and booing throughout.

Honestly, it's a mystery as to why this hasn't been brought back, beyond a few special episodes. Like *A Question of Sport*, the pop stars weren't always the most witty or articulate, but they clearly knew and cared about the subject. Much as I love *Never Mind the Buzzcocks*, it does sometimes feel like the pop stars are just there to be foils to the comedians or TV personalities – *Pop Quiz* gave them a chance to shine as their music-loving selves.

# IDEAS FOR MUSIC ROUNDS

It's difficult these days to find genres of music that everyone's into – any given crowd could have greater knowledge of pop, classical, country or drill. You've got to either cater to your particular crowd, or go super-general.

- For true musos: **Identify drum solos or guitar solos;** even harder than 'beat the intro' is 'identify the outro'!
- **Themed songs** – this way you can mix up eras and genres, but give people a chance of a lucky guess.
- **Song lists** – name as many of the people mentioned in 'We Didn't Start the Fire' or 'It's the End of the World as We Know It' as possible.

## Inspired by rounds on TV and radio

- Use some of our favourite rounds from Radio 4's *I'm Sorry I Haven't a Clue* – 'One Song to the Tune of Another' or 'Pick Up Song'. In the latter the player starts by singing along to the original recording which the quizmaster fades out and then fades back in; points are awarded for how close to time the singer is when the track comes back in.
- *Shooting Stars*' 'Club Singer' round – this one is very easy to do at home, the nominated player must perform a well-known song 'in the club style' and others must try to identify it despite the terrible rendition.

- Guess the intro – do it *Buzzcocks* style where you all have to hum, kazoo or otherwise vocalise the start of famous songs.

## Spotify game

Pick a song no one knows. You're given the title and artist, you get to look at the artwork, and then you have to sing the song as you imagine it. Then you check how close it is to the real thing.

## Question songs

You can either get the right answer or points for creative suggestions to the philosophical dilemmas posed therein?

- Why do fools fall in love?
- Who lives in a pineapple under the sea?
- What's another year?
- Do you know the way to San Jose?
- Where do broken hearts go?
- When will I be famous?

Play TikTok songs that you only know 30 seconds from, and you have to fill in the rest of the song.

Indentify sections of album covers – something you can't do so easily now!

## QUIZ – MUSIC

These are song titles expressed in other words. Can you guess the original name of the tune?

If these are proving a bit hard, you could give the name of the artist and – if you're feeling brave – sing the new lyrics to the tune of the original song.

1.  Farewell pathway to Oz (1973)

2.  In the fashion of one of Seoul's 25 government districts (2012)

3.  In a state of pleasing insensitivity (1979)

4.  Romeo Echo Sierra Papa Echo Charlie Tango (1967)

5.  Buddhist lizard (1983)

6.  Holy burning Muppet (fella dancing about) (1985)

7.  I can't get out (1985)

8.  I'm not a real fireplace (1955 / 1987)

9.  Where did I bloody well put it? (1987)

10. American landlord (1987)

11. Steps to a legendary London gay club (1971)

12. Incontinent Womble (1988)

13. Small, very small, scared, spotty cozzy (1990)

14. Dirty chemists (1964) (Could give a clue that it's also a film that came out in 2005)

15. Inflate the preserve (1989)

Obviously these songs are mostly from an earlier era (Lucy made them up and she's quite old), so why not have fun doing the same thing with more modern songs?

2

NAME ..................

SCORE ..............

1

NAME ..................

SCORE ..............

3

NAME ..................

SCORE ..............

THE
STAR PRIZE

## BRUCE FORSYTH, HOST OF *PLAY YOUR CARDS RIGHT*:

### *'What do points make? Prizes!'*

It's all well and good playing a quiz for quiz's sake. Yes, there is a lot to be said to finally beating your 12-year-old niece in a K-Pop showdown, but are you content with just the memory of her sulky face glowering at you for the remainder of her birthday party? No. WE WANT PRIZES.

Prizes add a layer to any competition. Literally, if you recall how furious you were when it wasn't you holding the 'pass the parcel' when the music stopped, meaning it wasn't you who nabbed the inter-layer bonus prize of a tiny yo-yo. The prize itself is often less relevant than the fact of its existence. Those contestants on *Bullseye* really wanted to win Bully's special prize – right up until they found themselves trying to tow a jet-ski back home down the A38 to Derby. What use is the prize dictionary to a *Countdown* Octochamp, other than to pop it in pride of place on the shelf above all your other dictionaries and point it out to every visitor who comes to tea? Prizes – we just want 'em.

In the early days of TV quizzing, the prizes were crap for

a good reason. The Independent Television Authority (later the Independent Broadcasting Authority) was the regulator for commercial TV companies, and they set a cap on how much money could be won on game shows. This had originally happened in response to the quiz show scandals in the US – we don't have time to explain those here, so your homework is to watch the 1994 movie *Quiz Show*. You'll thank me.

Producers tried to bring excitement and glamour to their shows by offering enticing consumer goods instead of cold, hard cash. Gen Z might find it laughable how thrilled we were at the idea of winning a TV 'WITH REMOTE CONTROL!!!' or an electronic clock radio. I couldn't even start to explain the Teasmade – a device that allowed you to sleep soundly, knowing that in the morning you'd be waking up to a freshly brewed cup of absolutely disgusting tea.

*The Generation Game* even had a conveyor belt of depressing prizes as the climax of the show. Contestants watched an array of sad items pass before their eyes, and then they won whatever they could remember – the selection always included a cuddly toy.

The prize money cap was only lifted when the IBA was abolished in the 1990s, allowing life-changing sums of money to be offered once more, and ushering in the epoch-defining *Who Wants to Be a Millionaire?*.

# WHO WANTS TO BE A MILLIONAIRE? Fact File

**NAME:** *Who Wants to Be a Millionaire?*
Named after the Cole Porter song from *High Society*, although most people are lazy and just call it *Millionaire*. The working title was *Cash Mountain*.

**DATES:** 1998 to 2014, then a short break, before returning from 2018 with a new host.

**CONCEPT:** Answer a series of increasingly hard questions to win a million.

**HOSTS:** Chris Tarrant and Jeremy Clarkson

**PRIZE:** Up to a million pounds. Only six people have taken the UK jackpot (at the time of writing). Judith Keppel was legendarily the first person to do so in 2000.

**CONTROVERSIES:** (Where do we begin?!)
The newspapers loved any scandal relating to *Millionaire*, because it was such a huge show.

Over the years there were many rumours of contestants trying to game the system. It became known that a syndicate of quizzers known as 'The Consortium' would help each other get on the show and win prizes, then split the cash.

The *Millionaire* show itself was accused of spoiling the finale of BBC show *One Foot in the Grave* by scheduling its first million-pound winner against it.

> Of course, the most famous event in the show's history was the 'coughing major' scandal that ended up in court cases, and a spectacular drama by James Graham. The TV version starred Michael Sheen, and we were lucky enough to interview him for our podcast.

## WHO WANTS TO BE A MILLIONAIRE?

So 1998 was the year that 'Can I phone a friend?', 'We don't want to give you that' and 'Is that your final answer?' entered the language.

The format of *Millionaire* was simple – basically, answer 15 general knowledge questions to win a million quid.

Everything about the show was perfect – a menacingly dark set with looping spotlights to ramp up the tension. Edgy music playing under the questions, with flourishing fanfares when things went well. Chris Tarrant was a brilliantly playful tormentor. His ability to draw out the answer reveal to agonising lengths has never been surpassed.

If you were around at the time, you'll remember what a cultural phenomenon this show was. We had the board game, tie-in book and even a chocolate version that I seem to remember was made by M&S. It even inspired a best-selling book (*Q & A*) which was adapted into the Oscar-winning movie *Slumdog Millionaire*. We eagerly await the film adaptation of *Going for Gold*.

The format and host have changed, but *Millionaire* is an enduringly popular show, and became a global smash hit. It was even credited with wiping out the slight queasiness around big money prizes that had haunted the US since the 1950s.

Certainly, being a talented quizzer in the States can be pretty lucrative these days. Quiz legends like Ken Jennings and Brad Rutter have won millions of dollars thanks to their efforts. *Jeopardy!* has been a huge payer for successful US quizzers, thanks to the fact that winners are allowed to return – Ken has won an amazing 74 times, and eventually was hired as a host.

*FUN FACT:* The biggest single prize ever bagged on British TV was £1,500,000. Graham Fletcher was the lucky man who took home the bumper pot on ITV's *Red or Black* in 2012. The show itself was essentially *Runaround* without the quiz, kids or Mike Reid, so we shall speak no more of it here.

Here in the UK we retain a certain fondness for slightly rubbish prizes. Even celebrities aren't immune to their charms. You'll have seen how desperately everyone fights to win the wheelie suitcase or the fondue set on *Richard Osman's House of Games.*

# RICHARD OSMAN'S HOUSE OF GAMES Fact File

**NAME:** *Richard Osman's House of Games*
You know you've arrived as a host when your name is in the official title of the show. Bob Monkhouse was such a legend that he didn't even use his full name for shows like *Bob's Full House* and *Bob's Your Uncle*.

**DATES:** 2017 to present

**CONCEPT:** Celebrities compete in really fun rounds that are at various points along the spectrum from quizzy to puzzly to parlour gamey.

**HOST:** Richard Osman. It's literally in the title.

**PRIZES:** In most celeb shows they're competing to win money for charity, but not here. Richard is a veteran game show producer, and prone to TV nostalgia himself, so he's recreated the kind of prizes we loved in the 1970s and 1980s. Fondue sets, toolboxes, bathrobes and so forth are up for grabs, and as a bonus they've got Richard's face on them.

**OUR FAVOURITE ROUND:** So many to choose from, but 'Where is Kazakhstan?' never fails to delight. It's such a simple premise – identify locations on a map, but it always proves incredibly tricky. You know every single person on the show has probably been to Greece, but can they find it on a map? No, they cannot.

## *RICHARD OSMAN'S HOUSE OF GAMES*

In TV it's normal practice to introduce a successful quiz show format, let it run for a few series, and then bring in a celebrity version. Once the brand is established, you'll find celebrities saying, 'Ooh, I'd love to have a go at *Tipping Point / The Chase / Pointless.*' *House of Games* has tipped all that on its head. It's a celebrity show that makes everyone want to become famous simply so they can appear on it. Never mind the champagne lifestyle, awards ceremonies, private jets and so forth, the real perk of being well known these days is that you get to compete for a toolbox with Richard Osman's facial features stuck on to it.

What makes this show so great? Obviously the prizes. But also, it's a really winning mixture of serious quizzing and silly little games. The fact that the players stay on all week gives you the chance to get to know them a little bit better. Sometimes the show throws up real shocks and surprises – like the time that *University Challenge* legend Bobby Seagull was beaten by Jay McGuinness from The Wanted. Jay is a man who conceals his huge brain and killer quiz instincts behind an extraordinarily sweet exterior.

The rounds are all expertly constructed to give the players a chance to have fun, but also show off their knowledge. In most panel games, the scoring doesn't count, as comedian Angela Barnes explained to us:

'The scoring could not be more arbitrary . . . I'm sure I'm not giving away any state secrets here but I do *Mock the Week* quite a lot, and people often say, "Oh, you're never on the winning team of *Mock the Week*," and I'm like, "Do you know in every episode we record both teams winning," and just by the luck of the draw, my team winning hardly ever makes the edit, but people feel really sorry for me, but no one's counting, it's fine.'

*House of Games* takes the fun chat from panel shows but raises the stakes for the players a little bit.

Richard Osman is a man who knows his way around a format – he devoted a large part of his life to devising and producing them before hopping in front of the camera. He's got a great eye for what works (*Pointless*) and what doesn't (*Shafted* with Robert Kilroy-Silk). We've all seen games and quizzes where you really enjoy them for one episode, but you get bored over a whole series, or the final round is really great, but you don't want to have to sit through the opening 25 minutes to get to it. The beauty of *ROHOG* is that it's a perfect home for ideas that are fun, but wouldn't really justify an entire half-hour.

With *House of Games*, there's a little bit of luck, but you generally feel that the week's winner deserved their trophy. The rounds have just enough variety to keep the show interesting, but because they're repeated it gives you a chance to find your favourite games and look forward to their reappearance.

Richard is a charming host, naturally, but he's also incredibly quick-witted. He's in charge of the show, his name's in the title, but he's gracious enough to sit back and let the talented people around him shine – and by that we don't just mean the players, we mean the producers and question setters. You can tell that he's enjoying himself playing along, and revelling in the creativity of his production team's ideas.

Richard is right that *House of Games* is a tribute to the skill of question writers. It's a properly challenging quiz. The questions and games on *ROHOG* are a little bit more challenging than the ones that celebrities usually face on TV (there's a tendency for celeb specials to have slightly, er, softer questions). The main thing that sets it apart though, is how funny it is. The end round, 'Answer Smash', makes you laugh every single day with its crazy juxtapositions of things, as you find yourself shouting 'Bolivia Newton-John!' at the telly.

## RICHARD OSMAN, HOST OF
## *HOUSE OF GAMES*:

'House of Games *is like a hymn to the art of the question writer. You've got all these lovely new and silly and funny ways of doing questions. We have all these brilliant ideas for shows and you think, "It's not a full show, it's just a round in a show," and on this one we just think great, let's do it. The real heroes of* House of Games *are the question writers.*'

**LUCY SAYS:**

The most admired items in my house are the prizes I've won on *Richard Osman's House of Games*. The dartboard is in constant use and everybody loves the sofa cushion! Last time I saw Richard I told him how much my friends enjoy sitting on his face, but he didn't seem that thrilled.

## QUIZZING AT HOME: PRIZES

### The *Millionaire* Model

Recreate the jeopardy of *Who Wants to Be a Millionaire?* by constructing your own prize ladder. Make it a ramp of chores and favours the winner can call in, from being made a cup of coffee, via sharing the Netflix login, all the way up to getting a lift to the airport for that 5am flight.

### Real *Jeopardy* for the quizmaster

In the US, they had *Win Ben Stein's Money*, which was remade over here as *Win Beadle's Money*. The quizmasters stood to lose something of theirs if the contestants won – which makes things really interesting. Maybe not money, though – play for a treasured possession (or not so treasured).

### Cabbages and Kings

Baffle anybody under the age of 40 by playing 'Double or Drop' from the chaotic children's classic *Crackerjack*. Sort of a quizzy buckaroo, contestants must answer questions while holding on to an ever-increasing pile of objects and prizes. If you get a question wrong, a cabbage is added to the pile (NB pre-warn your local greengrocer) and if you're out you walk away with only a pencil. Truly baffling.

### The honour is all yours

Sometimes you have to go with the purist side of quiz, and do it for the honour – or for a token of your superiority. Consider playing for the title of 'Monarch of the House' – entitling you to . . . well, just be officially the boss. One branch of my family started congratulating the winner of any game by calling out '*chapeau*', which is traditionally yelled at the victor in cycling (*chapeau* means 'hat' in French, essentially it means the same as doffing one's cap in respect). Over the years, this became a literal '*chapeau*' – a hat of victory that was placed on the winner's head and worn only by them until another game was played. Consider making a small ornament into your champion's trophy; you can even take photos of the award ceremony, and the winner retains the ornament until the next quiz.

## QUIZ – *WHO WANTS TO BE A MILLIONAIRE?*

We love the 'Prize Pyramid' structure of *Who Wants to Be a Millionaire?*. Here's a quiz with (we think) increasingly difficult questions. There are 15 questions here. You can start off with a small prize – such as one chocolate button – and ramp up the stakes as you go through the questions until by question 15 you're offering the star prize – as many Ferrero Rocher as you can fit in your mouth. Or whatever your family's equivalent of a million quid happens to be.

Feel free to let your family members gamble. You can have points at which you guarantee they won't walk away empty-handed (or empty-mouthed if you're giving away chocolate) and you can encourage them to gamble, just like they do in *Millionaire*. Enjoy yourselves with the catchphrases: 'You've won this commemorative tea towel from the Lake District, but we don't want to give you that . . .' It might be just the spur your contestant needs to go for the tin of Highland shortbread or fridge magnet from Filey. Enjoy!

**1. Which of these is an airport that serves New York City?**
JFK
OMG
LOL
BTS

**2. Which Disney princess is the main character in the movie _Tangled?_**

Tiana

Jasmine

Ariel

Rapunzel

**3. Which brand used the marketing phrase: 'It does exactly what it says on the tin'?**

Dulux

Ronseal

Fanta

Birds custard

**4. _Better Call Saul_ is a spin-off from which other TV show?**

_The Wire_

_The Sopranos_

_Breaking Bad_

_Succession_

**5. Which of these is NOT a breed of horse?**

Florida cracker

Belgian draught

Russian don

Irish setter

**6. In the UK, the abbreviation TUC can stand for Trades Union what?**

Congress

Council

Committee

Corporation

**7. What name is given to part of a sewing machine?**

Feed dog

Needle cat

Bobbin rabbit

Spool pigeon

**8. Which of these brands was founded most recently?**

Heinz

Hellmann's

Colman's

Lea and Perrins

**9. Which religion has a symbol called the Khanda?**

Buddhism

Sikhism

Jainism

Baha'i

**10. What is the meaning of the word eructation?**
Burping
Sneezing
Farting
Weeing

**11. Myology is a branch of medicine concerned with the structure and diseases of which parts of the body?**
Bones
Muscles
Ligaments
Nerves

**12. Often called 'the world's most southerly city', Ushuaia is in which country?**
Argentina
Chile
South Africa
Madagascar

**13. The Pritzker Prize is awarded in which discipline?**
Law
Accountancy
Psychiatry
Architecture

**14. In 1901 Edmund Barton became the first prime minister of which country?**
Canada
Malta
Australia
South Africa

**15. The Battle of the Coral Sea took place during which war?**
World War II
World War I
Boer War
Crimean War

# MEAN QUIZZES

## ADAM BOSTOCK-SMITH, WRITER ON
### *THE WEAKEST LINK*:
We spoke to Adam Bostock-Smith, who was the writer on the show who helped Anne come up with some of her cruel jibes. He said:

*'You'd do what they called the "who slaps" which were "who's the idiot in the pack?" or whatever, which she used to say at the end of each round. And then you'd have all the biographies of all the contestants, so I'd spend the night before going through all of those, and fishing out the little bits that she could be nasty to them about really!*
*'From my point of view, it never felt like you were really taking people apart. People knew exactly what they were getting into and I think they really enjoyed it. I don't think there was ever a case of anyone being properly offended.'*

Let us take you now to the darker side of quiz. A world of punishments, penalties, forfeits and general meanness.

To the dedicated quizzer, simply getting a question wrong is punishment enough, but TV formats sometimes demand that the losing contestant also gets humiliated.

In fact, in the early 2000s, watching people being insulted and belittled on TV was all the rage. Ritual mental torture was as fashionable as bucket hats, handkerchief tops and a little peek of thong poking out from the top of your boot-cut jeans.

The traditional quiz show host was kind, avuncular and – crucially – wanted the contestants to do well. Jim Bowen famously thought that everyone on *Bullseye* was 'super, smashing, great'. Even though Chris Tarrant could be a bit cheeky on *Who Wants to Be a Millionaire?*, we knew that deep down he always wanted to hand over the biggest cheque possible. Yes, Jeremy Paxman got exasperated with the teams on *University Challenge*, but he was just spurring them on to greatness. Also, no one really cared, because they were students.

That all changed with the arrival of *The Weakest Link* and Anne Robinson – the original mean girl of quizzing. From her terse catchphrase: 'You are the weakest link, goodbye' to the way she introduced the contestants: 'Which village is missing its idiot?' Anne was clearly not there to make friends.

## THE WEAKEST LINK
### Fact File

**NAME:** *The Weakest Link*

**DATES:** 2000 to 2012, then 2021 to now

**CONCEPT:** *Fifteen to One* meets *Big Brother*, overseen by a dominatrix. A circle of people answer questions to bank money. They vote each other off the show for being either too bad or too good. Last one standing wins the cash.

**HOSTS:** Anne Robinson and Romesh Ranganathan

**PRIZE:** Cash – contestants on the original series could win up to £10,000, quite a handsome sum for a daytime show. This was the era of *Who Wants to Be a Millionaire?* though, so splashing the cash was in vogue. In reality it was very hard to win much because people kept forgetting to shout 'bank!' at the right time.

**INSIDER VIEW:** As well as the classic catchphrases like 'You are the weakest link, goodbye!', *The Weakest Link* also featured different insults for the contestants each time. Some of these were aimed at the players in general when they were up for elimination:
'Who's the rotten tooth that needs to be pulled?'
'Who's the dark cloud with no silver lining?'
Some of the insults were very personal – for example, Anne, on hearing that a contestant was a professional beautician, said: 'Didn't have time to do anything on yourself today, then?'

★ ★ ★ ★ ★ ★ ★ ★ ★ ★ ★ ★ ★ ★ ★ ★ ★ ★ ★ ★

★ *FUN FACT:* **Anne Robinson can't say cutlery,** ★
★ **Antarctica or Greg Rusedski.** ★

★ ★ ★ ★ ★ ★ ★ ★ ★ ★ ★ ★ ★ ★ ★ ★ ★ ★ ★ ★

## NASTY NOUGHTIES

Reality TV shows like *Big Brother* were giving the public an appetite for seeing people being nasty to each other. *The Weakest Link* took the idea of making folk turn on one another and brought it to the quiz show format. It began with nine players, who would answer questions and then bank the money they'd won so far, up to a possible maximum of £10,000.

At the end of every round, players would nominate each other for elimination. Anne would helpfully point out who'd got questions wrong, who'd failed to bank money, or sometimes she'd just observe who had an annoying voice or an ugly shirt.

In the nasty noughties this was a massive hit, and for a while quiz and game shows with a bit of an 'edge' were everywhere. *Goldenballs* had a lovely, warm host in Jasper Carrott, but it provided the opportunity for cruelty by using the 'Prisoner's Dilemma'. This is a famous example of game theory where people have to choose whether to collaborate with each other for mutual benefit, or to betray each other for personal glory.

Other shows took a more standard format and just used an unpleasant host. Remember *Cleverdicks*? This Sky TV show suffered a bit by being made in 2012, the year *The Weakest Link* came off air, when people were really starting to tire of nastiness. It also suffered from being hosted by walking charisma vacuum Ann Widdecombe, seemingly for the sole purpose of making her say 'CleverDICK' a dozen times per episode. It only lasted one series.

Probably the most catastrophic failure of the 'cruel quiz' genre was *Shafted*, made in 2001 for ITV. This show cleverly combined both a combative format with a host nobody liked. The format was based on the 'Prisoner's Dilemma' (as used later in *Goldenballs*) and encouraged double-crossing. Robert Kilroy-Silk was a smarmy ex-MP who'd become famous for fronting a feisty daytime chat show posing charming questions like 'Could you live with a transvestite?' Or 'Are you 30, single and desperate?'

In other hands, the format of *Shafted* might have prospered. It had a clever little device where contestants had to bet money when given the teaser for the question that was about to come. So they'd hear 'Which planet . . .', and decide how much of their prize pot to bet that they could come up with the right answer. Then they'd hear the full question: 'Which Planet Hollywood investor starred in the 2000 remake of *Get Carter*'? And possibly regret their decision.

Contestants of course had the chance to vote each other off the show. Memorably Kilroy-Silk would ask players whom they wanted to 'Shaft', which was a bit awkward – kids, ask your parents. Then at the end, the last two players would vote to 'Share or Shaft'. If they both decided to share, they'd split the total prize pot between them, if one of them Shafted the other, the unscrupulous Shafter would get all the money. If they both Shafted each other then they went home empty-handed. This being in close proximity to the nasty noughties, chances were one or both of them would Shaft, meaning that the show ended with either both players, or the nicer person, leaving with nothing. As TV show finales go, it was bleak. I found it even more depressing than the final episode of *The Wire*, or the end of *Blackadder* where everyone dies.

In recent years, the fashion for back-stabbing viciousness seems to have abated. Even though the Chasers can be mean to contestants, lovely Bradley Walsh is there to soften the blow. Plus, we all know that the Chasers are lovely people in real life (Jenny threatened to give me a dead leg if I didn't put that).

Anne Robinson's sardonic style appeared to be less popular with the viewers of *Countdown* recently, and even *The Weakest Link* reboot with Romesh Ranganathan has toned down the hatred. Plus his viciousness is only directed at celebrities, and as we all know, they're fair game because they love the attention.

One feature of *The Weakest Link* was the 'Walk of Shame' – when a player was voted off, they were tracked by the camera as they stomped past Anne and off the set, before being bitter in a brief post-match interview. (In fact, contestants had to do the walk TWICE so they could get all the angles.) Executive producer Andy Rowe must have loved the Walk of Shame so much he based his next format all around the undignified departure – thus *101 Ways to Leave a Gameshow* was born.

The actual gameplay and questions on this show were vastly overshadowed by the 'Tower', the 100ft-tall purpose-built departure lounge for any contestants unlucky enough to come last in the round. On the whole, the 'ways to leave' ended with the player being pushed or dropped from height into a pool somehow; one stand-out involved host Steve Jones literally kicking the loser off the ledge while wearing a giant boot. There was only one UK series so we only saw 34 of the advertised 101 ways.

This was back in 2010, and seemed to round off the mean quiz trend. But is it making a comeback in the post-Covid era?

The psychological game show seems to be back on the up, with mind games taking the fore on shows such as *The Circle* (you can be anyone you want to be on social media – but can you maintain the persona?) and *The Traitors* (I AM 100 PER CENT FAITHFUL . . . honest . . .). Will the fashion continue into quizzing? Netflix unleashed their quiz *Cheat* in 2023, a format as much about blagging, bluffing and fibbing to the other players as it is about brains – very much *The Traitors* of quiz.

Are we returning to 'mean'? As long as that doesn't result in Ann Widdecombe getting another quiz show, I don't mind.

## SWEET CONSOLATION

Some quiz and game shows offer a trinket or memento for unsuccessful contestants. The TV equivalent of getting a participation certificate on school sports day, rather than a winner's medal or rosette. (I got a lot of certificates, but my mum told me they were actually better as they were easier to display on the wall. Thanks, Mum.)

Sometimes you wanted the consolation prize or booby prize more than the star prize. Examples of this include: the 'one year out' T-shirt on 'PopMaster', the *Blankety Blank* chequebook and pen, and a *Bullseye* Bendy Bully. But the best booby prize of all time for my money was that cheeky little fella Dusty Bin from *3-2-1*.

Oh, *3-2-1*. Unsurpassed in the mind-boggling quiz show stakes. Almost inexplicable. However, we will attempt to describe it here.

## 3-2-1 Fact File

**NAME:** *3-2-1*

**DATES:** 1978 to 1988

**CONCEPT:** Three couples were whittled down to two and then one. People did variety turns, and baffling cryptic clues were given. A robotic bin appeared every now and then.

**HOST:** Ted 'Fingers' Rogers – a stand-up comedian, but a lot more gentle than your Jim Bowens or Jim Davidsons. A big teddy bear really.

**PRIZES:** Big teddy bears. And other consumer goods, and holidays and cash. Most importantly, there was always the chance that contestants would walk away with only a little metal replica of Dusty Bin.

---

**FUN FACT: 3-2-1 was based on a Spanish show called *Un, Dos, Tres . . . responda otra vez* (*One, two, three . . . respond again*). This show ran in Spain from 1972 to 2004 and was MASSIVE! In the early years the British version imported most elements of the Spanish original – for example, each week was based around a theme like 'The French Revolution'. The Spanish equivalent of Dusty Bin was originally an enormous pumpkin called Ruperta. In Spanish the expression '*dar calabazas*' or 'give pumpkins' means to turn down someone's romantic overtures.**

---

MICHAEL SHEEN ON *3-2-1*:

'*3-2-1. It was like magic. There was something slightly sinister about it. It felt like I was watching something that was akin to a séance.*'

## 3-2-1

*3-2-1* was a ratings winner for ten years between 1978 and 1988. Its affable host Ted Rogers is remembered for his legendary hand gesture which went along with the title of the show. This gesture was then replicated in school playgrounds across the nation, and allowed you to accidentally-on-purpose stick two fingers up at your teachers ('flicking the Vs' as we called it).

As Ted Rogers said: 'It's a quiz, it's a game and it's big

variety,' and this Yorkshire TV production was a curious mixture of questions, cryptic clues and musical or comedy turns – but is best remembered for the head-scratching puzzles.

After some standard general knowledge questions to start, the star turns (actors, singers, comics, whoever was available that week) trotted out with an object to represent a prize on offer, and an accompanying clue. If the contestants could solve the clues, they could work out which prizes were worth choosing, with the star prize often being a holiday or a car.

But danger was afoot! The booby prize loomed large. One of the clues only pointed to Dusty Bin, the show's animatronic trash can mascot, and choosing that would send you home with a metal Dusty to gather dust on your dining room cabinet.

It's the cryptic nature of the clues that people remember more than anything. Sometimes the mental gymnastics involved in joining the dots were excruciating. Here's a classic example:

The object is 'A large wishbone' and the clue is:
'Take one that never changes, add a pub and a precious stone, bring them all up to date and now you're on your own.'

The logic here is
Large wishbone – comes from a large animal, something bigger than a chicken . . .
Take one that never changes – a 'constant'
Add a pub – in this case, an 'inn'
And a precious stone – an 'opal'

Constantinople being the old name for Istanbul, the prize was a luxury holiday to Turkey.

If you want to play along at home, here are some more:

Clue 1: Presented by dancer Jeff from the Alan Harding Dancers
American football: 'Handle this right and your score will show a nice touchdown. And you'll win five-o.'
(Turned out to be a holiday to Hawaii.)

Clue 2: Brian Conley
Hand cream: 'Don't fear those rainy showers erratic, both wet or dry they're automatic.'
(Turned out to be a compact laundry system, plus an ironing board and a dozen shirts.)

Clue 3: Cheryl Baker
Old style two-piece phone: 'You could get "canned" if that's your style, it sounds as if it's just your pile.'
(Turned out to be a stereo system.)

Clue 4: Roy Walker
An old-fashioned poke bonnet: 'A dash in this, a dash in that, it all depends what's under your hat.'
(Turned out to be a car!)

Clue 5: Johnny Moore from The Drifters

A used horseshoe: 'A tidy bit you will have won, if you take a tip at three to one.'

(Turned out to be Dusty Bin.)

## CRUELTY BEGINS AT HOME

Even though TV quizzing is less sadistic these days, sometimes a bit of jeopardy and the fear of failure is useful to raise the stakes, even when playing at home.

On telly, we don't mind watching people being given a hard time, but when you're playing with family, you might want to be a bit more careful. Remember whose roof you're under. If dad is cooking the Christmas dinner, do you really want to risk him giving you more sprouts than roast potatoes?

So, what kind of forfeits are acceptable when playing at home?

How about some inspiration from the world of kids' TV? Specifically the buckets of water from 1980s anarchy fest *Tiswas*.

If you're quizzing with young kids there's nothing they like more than seeing adults humiliated and, ideally, soaking wet.

We used to play a game with ours where someone would write down something that's a member of a category (i.e. 'colours of the rainbow' or 'vegetables') and fill a small plastic cup with water. Then the other players all had to say a colour until someone got the answer that was written down, at which point the entire cup of water was emptied over their head.

Of course, you also got drenched if you said a colour that

wasn't in the official rainbow, if you took too long to answer, or sometimes if the small child holding the water just got bored or held a grudge against you for not letting them have ice cream for breakfast that day.

Anyway, it's a great way to introduce younger children to quizzing. Things could get really tense if there were lots of members of the category and it went on for ages. The categories can be as simple and broad as you like – for instance, 'TV shows', 'shops on the high street' or 'members of this family' – and the general rule is that everybody must have heard of your answer.

We do not recommend playing this outside in midwinter, but it's a cracking summer pursuit.

For extra fun, and if it's a nice sunny day, you can empty the entire contents of a Super Soaker water pistol at the losers. You could even take direct inspiration from *Tiswas* and throw a whole bucket of water, singing 'The Bucket of Water Song'!

If you want to be horribly mean to the contestants in your quiz, there's a way to do it that doesn't involve making fun of their intelligence, appearance or personal hygiene. You can simply ask them fiendish or slightly misleading questions. The thing about a trick question is, when your contestants find out the answer they might say 'Genius! You really wrong-footed us with your brilliance there you clever old stick!' Or, more likely, they'll say 'Gah, that's so annoying/ factually misleading. You are a puffed up, arrogant clever dick. No one likes you and you smell of sprouts!'

## QUIZ – Mean Quiz

Here are a few examples of trick, or tricky, to use at your peril. Don't blame us if your family stops speaking to you altogether:

1. How many months have 28 days?

2. What is Paul McCartney's middle name?

3. On which continent would you find the world's largest desert?

4. In 2023, Niger was the country with the highest birth rate, but which country had the lowest birth rate?

5. In a typical jellyfish, which is bigger, its brain or its heart?

6. Which country has the longest border with France?

JET SET

HENRY KELLY ON *GOING FOR GOLD*:

'*We thought at first* [Going for Gold] *would last one year, because the original was based around the South Korean Olympics in Seoul.*'

## QUIZZING AROUND THE WORLD

It may feel like the UK is the home of the quiz, but they do it all over the world and often much better. In fact, the reigning World Quiz Champion, Ronny Swiggers, is from that hotbed of quizzing – Belgium. Is there a link between their pub culture and skill at general knowledge? I have already applied for a grant to 'research' this.

### *Chto? Gde? Kogda?* (What? Where? When?)

This evergreen quiz show has been hugely popular across the Russian-speaking world and former Soviet states since 1975, and created some of the first celebrity professional quizzers.

A panel of six quiz experts face crafty questions that have been submitted by viewers. The questions are often riddle-like and require the use of general knowledge alongside lateral thinking, meaning the experts must discuss as a team to solve the puzzle. Much like our own *Only Connect*, usually when the correct answer is revealed there are groans and recriminations and cries of 'gah, I should have got that' – a sign of a great question.

Most international versions of the show are made in

countries bordering Russia, although it was trialled in the USA in 2011 under the title *Million Dollar Mind Game* (presented, curiously, by our own Vernon Kay). Much more successful is the live competition version; it's estimated that around 50,000 teams take part in local, national and even international tournaments.

Sample questions:

In 2017, a construction company in Nizhny Novgorod hired a cat called Kefir, paying it a wage of 20,000 roubles (£170). What was its job?

(Answer: to cross the threshold. The constructors were building a block of flats; according to Russian folklore for good luck the first steps over a home's threshold should be a cat, and the bed should be placed wherever the cat lies down! The builders decided to impart the good luck to every flat. Kefir was busy!)

Since 1826, a street in Paris has had a name with a Russian association. However, the street has had its name changed three times. What is the name of the street?

(Answer: St Petersburg Street. The name was changed to match with the name of the Russian city – it became Petrograd Street in 1914, Leningrad Street in 1924 and St Petersburg again in 1991.)

What did the writer Viktor Pelevin describe as 'a virtual deodorant'?

(Answer: the smile emoji. Much like a deodorant makes you smell better, you can add the smiley face to anything, even a rude comment, and it looks like a joke.)

## QUIZZING ABOUT THE WORLD

TV quizzes traditionally offer fabulous holidays as prizes, and some of them even incorporate travel into the show itself. Here are some of our favourites:

### *The National Lottery: Jet Set*

This lovely little format, with bags of foreign glamour, graced our screens in the early 2000s. One of the games created to frame the drawing of the famous balls, it was one of the Lottery's more successful shows. Northern Irish powerhouse Eamonn Holmes was our host, and contestants could win the chance to live the life of an international jet-setter, in a winner-stays-on format.

The weekly champion stayed in the most luxurious resorts, was treated to once-in-a-lifetime experiences and given lavish spending money; then on Saturday night they'd have to play the studio challengers down the line from their five-star resort somewhere tropical in order to continue their trip.

One lucky winner stayed undefeated for three weeks and got to sample the delights of Tokyo, a South African safari and

Los Angeles before being dragged back to the UK. No news about whether their employer was particularly happy about the situation.

## *Busman's Holiday*

Despite the depressing title – a 'busman's holiday' is where you go away but still end up doing activities related to your everyday job – this was a jolly show that ran for eight series between 1985 and 1993.

Teams were made up of folk from the same job sector – for instance, florists, puppet animators, greyhound tic-tac men and fishmongers. Yes, plenty of professions that don't even exist any more. They faced questions about geography, their jobs and the jobs of the opposing teams in order to win a holiday.

Here's the hook – when they reached their destination, they went to see how their jobs were done elsewhere in the world, and the video of their adventures was broadcast the following week, when they returned to have another shot at a busman's holiday in a different location. It was hosted variously by Julian Pettifer, Sarah Kennedy and Elton Welsby.

The questions were pretty tough and very specific. For example:

*Survival Experts:*
Below what core temperature is someone clinically suffering from hypothermia?
35 degrees

*Genealogists:*
In whose reign was the act for the registrations of births and deaths introduced?
Queen Victoria

*Golf Club Secretaries:*
There are four circumstances listed in the rules of golf under which a player can discontinue play. Can you list two of them?
 Illness, danger from lightning, if the committee has suspended play, to get a ruling on a disputed point.

The lovely thing about this show was the fact that it gave you a glimpse into different professions. A team of genealogists from Ipswich won an all-expenses-paid trip to Belgium to visit an archive. The resulting film is a solid three minutes of middle-aged women looking at documents, and I love it! You don't get entertainment like that these days (outside of *Who Do You Think You Are?*)

## Where in the World?

This swish show was hosted in 1971 by Michael Parkinson, and then in the 1980s by impressionist Ray Alan. Contestants – a mixture of celebrities, travel experts and beauty queens (generally a well-travelled bunch) – would answer geography questions, sample international delicacies and generally show off about how cosmopolitan they were.
 This series wouldn't be of much note except for this one

fun fact – it was thanks to *Where in the World?* that Michael Caine got together with his wife Shakira Baksh. He spotted her as a panellist on the programme (having fancied her in an advert) and got in touch with the producers to get her number. Mildly creepy, but it all worked out very happily in the end – they celebrated their 50th wedding anniversary in 2023.

### Turner Round the World

In this 1997 show, viewers phoned in to win a dream holiday if they could correctly identify the mystery location that Anthea was visiting this week. The viewers could win a single trip, but Anthea got an entire series' worth. That woman is no fool!

## GOING FOR GOLD
## Fact File

**NAME:** *Going for Gold*

**DATES:** 1987 to 1996 and briefly revived in 2008/09

**CONCEPT:** Quizzers from all over the world (but mostly Europe) compete to win a prize that's loosely themed around 'Gold'.

**HOSTS:** Henry Kelly, David Suchet

**FUN FACT:** Given the added difficulty for people with a different first language, and the fact that England, Wales, Scotland and Northern Ireland were classed as separate nations, you'd expect the UK contestants to have romped home every time, right? Wrong. UK nationals won only three of the original nine series. Belgium was the second most successful nation, with two winners, tied with England. The format of *Going for Gold* was borrowed to create *One to Win* for Channel 5 in 2000. This featured Robin Houston, who is referenced elsewhere in this book as the mysterious, unseen host of *100%*.

## GOING FOR GOLD

We couldn't mention the world of international quizzing without talking about this iconic quiz, one of our favourite shows of all time.

This knockout quiz contest was originally commissioned to tie in with 1988 Seoul Olympics – hence the name, and the logo resembling a gold medal. The series champion received a trip to the Olympics in South Korea, which seemed impossibly glamorous to us armchair quizzers (die-hard quiz fans will know that the trip was won by one Daphne Fowler, serial quiz champion and former Egghead). Subsequent series offered similarly gold-themed prizes, such as a holiday to gold-prospecting territory in Australia.

A variety of factors came together to make this a truly classic quiz show:

1. Hans Zimmer's banging theme tune.
2. Our host Henry Kelly – a man who cannot be described in any way other than 'twinkly'. Formerly a hard-hitting journalist in his native Ireland (he wrote extensively on The Troubles), he made a conscious decision to leap into light entertainment, first as a host on *Game for a Laugh* before finally finding his quiz show niche with *Going for Gold*.
3. The contestants were from various European nations, but the questions were in English – meaning that most quizzers were competing in their second or third language. This inherent unfairness meant that it was even more impressive when this was overhauled and Erik from Norway knocked out Janet from England and Ray from Scotland.
4. The round formats. Round one featured long-form questions – Henry would ask 'Who am I?' or 'What am I?', then launch into a paragraph of clues about the person/object which would become increasingly obvious (quizzers' note: this is known as 'pyramidal' in quiz circles) until someone buzzed in with the correct answer. The final round featured some very impressive graphics

showing who had control of the question and how many points it was worth. Quite dramatic, and mildly baffling.

5. The set design was an ode to pastel – a classic 1980s look, contrasted with the modern trend for 'dark floor' sets.

★ ★ ★ ★ ★ ★ ★ ★ ★ ★ ★ ★ ★ ★ ★ ★ ★ ★ ★ ★ ★

**FUN FACT: The format was based on a long-running French series called *Questions Pour un Champion* (my A level French allows me to translate this as Questions for a Champion). It's a domestic series so they don't expect Janet from England to join in – however, they have had a special series featuring contestants from various Francophone nations.**

★ ★ ★ ★ ★ ★ ★ ★ ★ ★ ★ ★ ★ ★ ★ ★ ★ ★ ★ ★ ★

## 🎤 HOST WITH THE MOST: Henry Kelly

Henry Kelly was a respected journalist, who authored the seminal work *How Stormont Fell* in 1972 about The Troubles. He moved to London and worked as a journalist for BBC Radio 4. Inspired by family friend Terry Wogan, Kelly moved into light entertainment presenting and was one of the pranksters on stools in ITV's *Game for a Laugh* along with Jeremy Beadle, Sarah Kennedy and Matthew Kelly (no relation).

Henry freely admitted to us that he had no particular interest in becoming a quiz show host, but his journalism chops paired with his light ents experience made him a dependable choice for *Going for Gold* and he held it together with aplomb.

Like all the greats, he mixed a flair for facts with being a good people person. He always had a fact at his fingertips about the contestants' nations to make them feel at ease. His catchphrases like 'Who am I?' And 'Hans, you're playing catch-up' were somehow funny. He was a huge hit with the student population, who watched this show hung-over.

## QUIZ – JET SET

Here are a selection of questions, some of them about towns (mostly about Britain), and some about countries (mostly about the rest of the world). You could mix these up in the same round or do them as separate rounds. Or you could ask your contestants whether they'd rather have a town question or a country question, depending on whether they're more confident in their global or local geography.

### Town Questions

1. Aquae Sulis was the Roman name for which British town?

2. The town of Oswestry is in which British county?

3. The Metrocentre shopping centre is in which English town?

4. In which county is the town of Skegness?

5. Which town is the county town of Somerset?

6. In which fictional town is *Coronation Street* set?

7. Which of the Wombles is named after a town on the Isle of Mull?

8. What is the capital town of the Isle of Man?

9. The towns of Hamilton, London and Windsor are all part of which Canadian province?

10. The name of which North African capital city means 'three towns'?

11. The French town of Montelimar is famous for the manufacture of what sweet treat?

12. In which Buckinghamshire town is the Open University based?

**Country Questions**

1. The country of Bangladesh was known by what name between 1955 and 1971?

2. Which country uses the internet domain extension .jm?

3. Eden Park is a cricket ground in which country?

4. Which country's currency is the ringgit?

5.  Kigali is the capital of which African country?

6.  Until 1993, Eritrea was part of which other African country?

7.  Of which country is Lusaka the capital?

8.  'Pho' is a type of soup originating from which country?

9.  In which European country is the beach resort of Albufeira?

10. In which country was Florence Nightingale born?

11. Vilnius is the capital of which Baltic country?

12. Chile declared its independence in 1818 from which country?

13. Which is the largest sovereign country with no land borders?

14. From which country does the beer Pilsner Urquell originate?

15. Which is the only country with wild Komodo dragons?

16. In which country is the Aswan Dam?

2

NAME .................
SCORE .................

1

NAME .................
SCORE .................

3

NAME .................
SCORE .................

10

HOW TO HOST YOUR OWN QUIZ

## RICHARD OSMAN ON PANEL SHOWS
## AND QUIZ SHOWS:

*'Comedy panel shows, they're sort of quizzes; we ask questions, we have points. They don't matter particularly, but equally they do matter because you're giving a narrative that goes from the start to the end which is, "We're going to ask some questions and someone's going to win."*
*'And comedy always needs context, that's what a panel show is. It's kind of giving that quiz magic dust to stand-ups. With quiz, the format has to be far more developed, and the format is absolutely the thing. It's not just a platform for people to be entertaining, it's more like a sport with a set of rules. But now there are shows – like* House of Games *I would argue – which is sort of a mix between the two. It's a real quiz, and it's [a] serious quiz, but it has the bones of a show where you want people to be entertaining and chat to you and have a laugh with you.'*

It's often not until you're tasked with writing a quiz that you realise it's not always a straightforward job. It's definitely not as easy as doing a quick internet search for 'quiz questions' and hoping for the best . . .

A good quiz should be thoughtful and crafted for the occasion, something that will please everyone and – essentially – be accurate. I've been there as a quiz host – your heart sinks as you start to read out a question and you realise there's a mistake in it, it's out of date or, worst of all, there's a blank space where the answer should be. Which is why I always like to write my own, and if I can't, I always check the questions before starting the quiz.

We've dotted some questions for your use throughout this book, but you'll need more, won't you, you quiz addict? Here are a few tips on writing and compiling your own quizzes.

## GET INSPIRED

You've got to have a starting point – try the day's newspaper and think up at least one question for each page, from the big news stories through to sport, via horoscopes, TV listings and even the advertisements. That should give you a nice range of topics, plus you're very up to date. Same goes for looking at, for instance, the front page of Wikipedia – there's always an article of the day, plus a load of links to subjects that are in the news.

There's also no harm in using quiz books or the question cards in board games as a jumping off point. Just take a bit of care and double-check the information – if you're still using the original edition of Trivial Pursuit, then some facts are liable to have changed since 1981, so beware.

## KEEP IT VARIED

Unless it's a specialist subject quiz, then including a variety of topics is essential for keeping every player engaged. Covering your bases across your 'classic' subject areas – history, geography, science, the arts, sport etc. – means there will be a little chance for everyone to have a go, and you'll get to slot in lots of other subjects in between.

Also consider keeping the answers varied. You'll notice when watching TV quiz shows that it's very rare for the answer to be a name, or a colour, several times in a row. The question writers for telly are even picky about using similar subjects within the same episode – you won't get questions mentioning, say, Disney, or Paris, twice in a show.

## CHECK IT OUT

Consider taking time to double- or triple-check your quiz. The last thing you want as a quizmaster is to get into a dispute over an answer, when you should all just be enjoying yourselves. On broadcast quizzes, questions will go through several rounds of checks and verifications before they can be used, with multiple reliable sources cited for each fact. Obviously you don't need to be quite so thorough with a quiz at home or work – after all, you're not playing for thousands of pounds like on *The Chase* or *Pointless* (well, fewer thousands on *Pointless*) – but it will make for a more comfortable time as a quiz host if you know you can rely on your questions completely.

Also, verifying means you have the total authority to dismiss any smart-alec challenges; a very satisfying feeling.

## TAILORING TO YOUR AUDIENCE

You can have fun putting together your quiz when you know who is playing. You can pop a little treat in there for each member of your family or friend group – a question on a topic they love will give them the chance to shine and feel smart. If you have a spread of ages and generations then try and cover every era; on the other hand, if you know you are setting a quiz for teenagers then don't bother asking about the Suez Crisis or the Smash robots.

Remember, not everybody is a 'quizzer', but everybody likes to contribute and it's always a thrill to help get the right answer. Consider asking cryptic questions that need to be worked out, or even practical ones to guess or work out – e.g. How many jars are there on the kitchen shelf? Photo/picture rounds are also a good leveller – some people absolutely love them but are not so good at the rest of the quiz – the same goes for a music round.

It may also be that your family are serious *University Challenge*-level quiz buffs, but your work colleagues are . . . not. Don't subject them all to the same questions – nobody wants to feel thick at a quiz. If in doubt, make your questions easier by adding in clues. A rule of thumb – in a round of ten questions, you would like to see most teams get seven or eight, with the winners getting nine or maybe ten and no teams getting below five (unless it's the last round and there has been wine), so err on the side of easiness.

Keep bearing in mind that you want everyone to have a bit of fun and not feel alienated. It's a tricky task, making everyone feel entertained, valued and happy, so we doff our caps to the people who write questions and compile quizzes week in, week out.

## CHEATING

In some households this is a banned word, just like 'stupid' or 'Ann Widdecombe'. Some people think of it simply as 'bending the rules'. In my family, it's known as 'mee-mawing' – a phrase with a dark history going back to a particularly vicious round of charades at New Year 1981, on which we shall not dwell.

The thing is, cheating will happen. Or at least someone will try to 'bend the rules' to their benefit. If you account for this one way or the other, you'll have a less stressful quiz.

### Ways to stamp out cheating

1. Minimise earwigging and swan-necking

Two more terms from the ultra-competitive Ryan household. Earwigging is the act of trying to overhear what other teams are discussing; swan-necking comes from craning one's neck to glimpse what your opponent is writing down. Tip: earwigging is not so easy when there is some background music playing. It's more down to the players to make sure the oppos can't see their papers, but using a clipboard or a book to lean on means you can angle the paper away.

## 2. Penalise them

If you're a strict QM, then dock points when you suspect funny business.

If you're running a larger-scale event – such as a charity workplace quiz – then make it a financial penalty. Any teams caught using their phones mid-round must make a donation to the charity of the day. You can bet that everyone will have eagle eyes on their opponents, and won't hesitate to tell tales. I usually set the bar at £50 – that's chunky enough to be a deterrent, but also means if the CEO gets drunk and decides to look up a few answers then the charity will benefit nicely.

## 3. Minimise the opportunity to consult Uncle Search Engine

Isn't it funny how someone can wander off to the loo around question 40, and suddenly be inspired to remember the answers to questions 2, 5 and 9? To avoid this, short, sharp rounds are where it's at. Ideally, ten questions, then the answer sheets must be handed in at the same time.

Quizzers at home can mark each other's papers – but do you really trust them to mark their own?

At larger events it's much more efficient to collect the papers in and mark them yourself, or with an assistant. You can keep track of scores and also see what the most common or funniest wrong answers are. It also keeps the event running more smoothly, especially if your quizzers are having a few drinks.

## Ways to work with the cheating instinct

### 1. Hints

Every player or team has a hint token which they can cash in. The quizmaster can either just tell them the answer (boring) or give them some massive clues until they work it out (much more fun). Just watch out for the other quizzers trying to earwig! If you're running a charity quiz, you can even sell hint tokens to raise additional funds.

### 2. The Ungoogleable becomes Googleable

If you think a player might be tempted to use their phone for an answer, this would be a great way to catch them out . . .

Ask questions where nobody is likely to know the actual answer – most often with numerical answers where players are just giving their best guess, for instance:

- What is the current population of Reading?
- When is the next full moon?
- How many days until Halloween?

You can then use your smart speaker to be your official adjudicator by asking it directly – this minimises the margin for arguing the toss over the answer, and means the answer will be absolutely up to date.

## 🎤 HOSTS WITH THE MOST

Hosting a quiz show is definitely more than just reading out questions from a card (20th century) or iPad screen built into a podium (21st century).

Yes, that's your main job, but there are a lot of moving parts in a quiz. Firstly, you have to make the contestants feel relaxed and at ease (or terrified and on edge if that's the vibe of the show). You have to make sure that the rules are adhered to and that all is fair and above board. If you're on TV you might have the director and producers talking into your ear, maybe a studio audience to keep engaged, as well as the audience watching at home.

The best hosts make all this look easy, and in this book we have mentioned quite a few of them.

We can think of a few examples of perfectly good formats that have been let down by shoddy presenting, but we're too polite to name them here. We can also think of some flimsy premises for shows that have been elevated by a charismatic host. Again, we're not going to name them, but if you ever meet us in real life, slip us a fiver and we'll spill all.

On our podcast we've been lucky enough to interview Henry Kelly, Les Dennis, Richard Osman, Ben Shephard, Rick Edwards, Tim Vine and more. They've all been sweetly humble about their skills, but we think that they deserve all the plaudits.

We've spoken about a number of hosts throughout this book, but here are some of our other favourites, in no particular order:

### Bob Monkhouse

From *The Golden Shot* to *Wipeout*, Bob had the golden touch when it came to quiz and game shows. Pure showbiz, he was sometimes teased about being smarmy or insincere, but the public could tell that he loved the shows he fronted and cared about the contestants. He was legendary for the care he took to remember the names of everyone involved in the productions he worked on. He was also a brilliant gag writer, a gifted cartoonist and a walking encyclopedia of comedy.

### Clive Myrie

Clive has rapidly achieved national treasure status, and part of that must be down to his cool, calm, authoritative hosting of *Mastermind*. John Humphrys had done such a fantastic job for years that it was impossible to imagine anyone else in the role, but Clive stepped up and won our hearts.

### Bradley Walsh

It's impossible to resist Bradley's cheeky charm. No other quizmaster gets fits of the giggles so frequently and so delightfully. He's always on the side of the contestants on *The Chase* and *Beat the Chasers*, but his ribbing of the Chasers stays on the right side of rudeness. He's also the latest in a line of phenomenal *Blankety Blank* hosts. It's no coincidence that stand-up comics often make great hosts for quiz shows. When you face hostile stag nights in comedy clubs you learn to think on your feet. Bradley's also excelled as an actor, singer and sportsman, which has given him the wealth of experience and knowledge he brings to the best show on television (not that we're biased).

### Alexander Armstrong

If we're including Bradley, then we can't miss out his teatime rival, Xander. These two may be pitted against each other on different TV stations, and their accents are a world apart (or at least a few counties apart), but they're cut from the same cloth. Unfailingly good-natured, generous and supportive, Xander exemplifies the first rule of hosting – the show only exists because of the contestants, so make sure they're the true stars. He also loves to play along himself, and doesn't mind admitting when he gets the answers wrong. Like Bradley, he's also an actor, singer and all-round good guy. He makes the show feel like a delightful party to which we've all been invited.

### Ken Bruce

We couldn't list our favourite hosts without giving a nod to radio. There are so many great presenters working in the medium of audio. Honourable mentions to Paul Gambaccini for *Counterpoint*, the music quiz, Kirsty Lang on *Round Britain Quiz* and Russell Davies for *Brain of Britain*. We're choosing to focus on Ken Bruce because 'PopMaster' is so iconic, and because Lucy is frankly obsessed with him. Whenever another presenter had to stand in for Ken during his Radio 2 years, you could hear the terror in their voices as they realised how hard it was to manage this apparently simple game. Ken had brilliant banter with the callers and kept the good ship 'PopMaster' sailing smoothly. The TV version on Channel 4 has been a delight too.

# #BEKIND

It's very easy to mock people when they give a wrong answer. In fact, the internet is full of compilations of 'stupidest answers on TV game shows', newspapers regularly run lists of hilarious gaffes, and the magazine *Private Eye* often features quiz show contestants in its 'Dumb Britain' section.

We've both been contestants, and of course a big fear is giving an answer that's so monumentally wrong it passes into the annals of history. Social media has ensured that your moment of brain freeze will be captured and shared endlessly, so the stakes have never been higher for those who venture into the spotlight.

However, we always say that it's better to give a wrong answer than no answer at all. Sometimes you can venture a guess that turns out to be right, and there's no sweeter feeling.

Also, most of the people who direct vitriol and ridicule towards quiz show contestants would never have the guts to get up and do it themselves. Unless you've experienced the blind terror of being quizzed under the harsh glare of studio lighting, you have no business making fun of those who've given it their best shot.

Sometimes the wrong answers are simply adorable, like the woman on *Family Fortunes* who was asked what 100 people would have answered to the question 'Name something red' and said 'My cardigan'.

One of the main jobs of a game or quiz show host is being kind when people say idiotic things, and our favourite,

**Les Dennis,** is an absolute master of that art.

During his tenure as host of *Family Fortunes* he even had a catchphrase entirely for this situation: 'If it's up there I'll give you the money myself.'

Other legendarily kind hosts include:

**Roy Walker** – The inventor of the *Catchphrase* catchphrase 'Say What You See'. Softly spoken and gentle, Roy proved that you didn't need to be brash and bombastic to be a big hit on primetime. He was also so kind, sometimes in the face of some truly extraordinarily bad guesses. 'It's good, but it's not right' is such a lovely way of saying 'You're wrong, you fool!'

**Ben Shephard** – *Tipping Point* has become quite notorious for funny wrong answers. Ben regularly delivers a masterclass in keeping a straight face when a contestant is saying something spectacularly dumb.

**OUR FAVOURITE . . .**

OUR OWN SILLY MOMENTS

**LUCY:** On the podcast, I once asked 'What was the name of the ship in *Mutiny on the Bounty*?'

**JENNY:** I will never live down not being able to calculate the answer to 'How many is six dozen?' in a final chase.

## HOW TO BE A GOOD QM*

We've seen there are many ways to host a quiz, from strict headteacher to jokey best mate. Use whatever persona you wish, inspired by those we've discussed – but here are some tips on maintaining complete quiz control.

### Who's the boss?

Heavy is the head that wears the crown. As a child I wondered why my grandad – the best of all of us at quizzes – always took the role of QM. I now understand. It quashed arguments before they started. See, if you are known as the alpha quizzer of the group, whichever team you are not playing on will cry foul – even if the teams are drawn randomly. By coincidence, I now find myself taking on the mantle of QM to avoid any howls about unfairness.

### My house, my rules

Explain the rules at the beginning, keep consistent and you will keep the game running smoothly. My family are particularly bad for overruling a QM if they show any sign of weakness – there will be appeals for stewards' enquiries, arguing the toss over answers and protestations about the rules not being clear. I feel like Premier League referees should have to face their complaints as part of their training, they are that overwhelming. The QM should have their game plan in place, have an answer for everything (usually 'no') and should not allow whingeing to pause the game. Your decision is final.

## My fair QM

Ideally, the QM should be completely neutral, but try finding someone like that on Boxing Day. Don't play favourites. Or at least don't make it obvious.

## Alexa, add up the scores

In the olden days of game shows, the (male, always male) host would be assisted by a much younger and rather glamorous lady. Now, the role is much more likely to be a tall nerdy chap in a suit. Either way, an assistant is extremely useful to have by your side as a QM. At home, they can help keep scores, watch out for cheating and pass out pens and paper; if you're in charge of a larger quiz at work or school then they can take in the answer sheets and mark them while you concentrate on hosting duties. This is an ideal role for a family member who might not be as keen on taking part but still wants to be involved in the game.

*This traditionally stands for Quizmaster or Quizmistress but it really can stand for whatever you like – e.g. Quizmonster, Quizmangler, Quizmaniac. Just as long as it denotes that the holder of the title is 'in charge of the quiz'.

## OUR FAVOURITE . . .

### SIDEKICKS AND ASSISTANTS

We think quiz show hosts are superheroes, and these days they're just as likely to have a helpful and entertaining sidekick in support. You could see Alexander Armstrong as a posh Spiderman, with Richard Osman as his literal 'guy in the chair'. Actually, come to think of it, Xander's more like Bruce Wayne, with Richard as his Alfred – delivering facts on a silver salver – or his Robin because he always wears tights behind that desk (not sure this superhero analogy is really going to sustain much longer if I'm honest).

Traditionally, hosting a quiz was seen as man's work. If a woman was allowed any role on a quiz or game show, it was generally that of 'lovely assistant'. The host would tackle the serious business, but he might have a glamorous lady or two on hand to do the fluffy work of making the contestants feel at ease, draping herself languidly across a car bonnet, or showing us how to load a washing machine.

The received wisdom was that the audience wanted to think that the host knew all the answers, and they simply wouldn't believe that we girls had space in our head for general knowledge alongside all the recipes and make-up tips.

Thankfully that nonsense seems to be on the way out, and the nature of the sidekick's duties have changed markedly over the last few decades.

Here are some of our favourite assistants:

## ISLA ST CLAIR

*The Generation Game* always had a woman to wrangle the contestants and provide a foil for the host. These women always had a lot going on behind the light entertainment permasmiles. After being queens of the conveyor belt, many of them became incredibly successful in various fields. Rosemary Ford went on to present *Come Dancing*, Dee Ivens is a kick-ass personal trainer, and Lea Kristensen is an eminent psychotherapist.

We loved Isla St Clair on *Gen Game*, because she had such a warm chemistry with Larry Grayson. We knew enough about Larry to realise that she was unlikely to get married to him like Anthea Redfern had done with Brucie. The affection between Larry and Isla was genuine and wholesome, and he allowed her the space to shine. Isla had been a folk singer before she took on the hostess role, and she has subsequently devoted her life to discovering, cataloguing and playing traditional Scottish tunes. She's now a leading music historian, and we are delighted for her. We look back fondly on Larry's evident devotion to 'My lovely Isla, my Saturday girl'.

## THE DOLLY DEALERS

In the case of *Play Your Cards Right*, they had a whole gang of glamorous women, and often a lone man for the sake of balance. Bruce Forsyth – always king of the catchphrase – even had a little rhyme especially for them:

'And here they are, they're so appealing, OK dollies, do your dealing!'

While they were undoubtedly objectified, the thing we

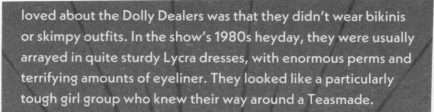 

loved about the Dolly Dealers was that they didn't wear bikinis or skimpy outfits. In the show's 1980s heyday, they were usually arrayed in quite sturdy Lycra dresses, with enormous perms and terrifying amounts of eyeliner. They looked like a particularly tough girl group who knew their way around a Teasmade.

### CAROL VORDERMAN

*Countdown* has always had a slight overstaffing issue. There are only two contestants, but they've always been outnumbered. On the first episode of the show in 1982, along with Richard Whiteley hosting, we had farmer celebrity farmer Ted Moult with lexicographer Mary in dictionary corner, Cathy Hytner picking out the letters, Beverley Isherwood picking out the numbers and Carol Vorderman doing the sums. The producers eventually realised that Carol was more than capable of multitasking, and she went on to be the sole regular co-host until 2008.

Carol's lightning mental arithmetic took the nation by storm and – along with Johnny Ball – she joined the ranks of Britain's most loved mathematicians. Her presence on the show inspired generations of girls to embrace maths, and she passed the torch to Rachel Riley. We should also give a huge shout out to Susie Dent, whose excellence with etymology and flair for philology have similarly motivated us all to think a bit more deeply about the language we use every day.

### CAROL SMILLIE

Carol rose to fame in *Wheel of Fortune*. At first she didn't have a huge amount to do, but she was always a warm and calming presence on the show. Her natural charm was evident – she became known as 'Smiley Smiley Carol Smillie' through Ronni Ancona's impression of her. She was the very definition of 'more than just a pretty face' and quickly became a phenomenally successful TV presenter, as well as a musical theatre actress, a pioneer in the field of period underwear, and latterly a humanist celebrant!

## JOHN VIRGO

*Big Break* was a hugely popular snooker-based quiz of the 1980s. John Virgo was the resident expert on the baize, and his trick shots were the absolute highlight of the show. He also provided a laid-back and sardonic contrast to Jim Davidson's manic energy.

**FUN FACT:** Lucy bought an original John Virgo waistcoat and bow tie from a *Big Break* winner on eBay. We've now given it away to a podcast listener, so keep your eye on our social media for chances to win other incredible artefacts like that.

## VANNA WHITE

The American forerunner of Carol Smillie, Vanna White joined the American original *Wheel of Fortune* as hostess in 1982. That show is the longest running syndicated game show in the United States, and Vanna is still right there. She's won a Guinness World Record for 'most frequent clapper', as they estimated she'd clapped on the contestants a staggering 3,721,446 times over 32 series of the game. America was seized by 'Vannamania' when she first appeared, and they're in no hurry to find a cure for it.

## SOME OTHER HONOURABLE MENTIONS:

- **Alex Horne** on *Taskmaster*
  Little Alex Horne devised the show, keeps it on track and withstands quite vicious abuse from Greg.
- **Matt Lucas** as George Dawes on *Shooting Stars*
  The most entertaining way we've ever seen scores delivered; by a massive baby with a drum kit.
- **Anneka Rice** on *Treasure Hunt*
  Kenneth Kendal was the official host of *Treasure Hunt*, but the show was always more about Anneka and her jumpsuits.
- **Samantha** on Radio 4's *I'm Sorry I Haven't a Clue*
  She may be fictional, but we've all got a warm place for Samantha in our bosoms. The innuendo-laden sign-offs are legendary:
  'Samantha tells me she has to go now as she's off to the country residence of her new gentleman friend, who has some interesting birds in the thicket. He keeps a young chicken, but Samantha says there are also wild breeds there, and she can't wait to see his woodcock, pullet and swallow.'
- **The Banker** on Channel 4's *Deal or No Deal*
  Another unsung and unseen hero. There was wild speculation about the identity of this mysterious money

man. We always thought it was Elvis or Lord Lucan, but he was eventually revealed to be the show's executive producer (and ex-*Corrie* actor) Glenn Hugill.

- **Mr Chips** on *Catchphrase* and **Mr Babbage** on *Family Fortunes*
  These were delightfully low-tech early computer sidekicks. Presumably now there'll be a slew of AI-generated assistants – yet another way in which the robots are coming for our jobs.

We've loved reminiscing about our favourite TV quiz and game shows, and we hope it's been a pleasant trip down memory lane for you, too. Or, if you're a youngster, we trust you haven't been too baffled by our constant references to Teasmades and Jim Bowen. We regard these shows as beacons of light among the gloom of news, current affairs, gritty police dramas and true crime documentaries. We love all those genres, as well as reality shows, sitcoms, cooking shows, singing/dancing shows, magazine programmes and *The Repair Shop* (oh boy do we love *The Repair Shop*) but a good quiz scratches the itch for knowledge that burns within us all.

Our main aim, the thread that runs through everything we do on our podcast, is to inspire our listeners to seek out facts and enjoy sharing them with others. Like Jenny's grandad and Lucy's dad, we want to encourage a thirst for learning. We hope you can use what we've shown you to create memorable moments with your friends and families. Whether you're the question setter, the host, the helpful sidekick, or you just want to make up a theme tune for your quiz and sing it full-throatedly, we hope this book has furnished you with some ideas.

Before we leave you, we thought we'd give you a few more sample rounds that you might like to use. There are some new concepts, as well as rounds of classic general knowledge trivia questions. Feel free to adapt them, reword them, or even correct them if you think we've got anything wrong – remember if it's your quiz, your decision is final and trumps even our authority. Above all, have fun and get quizzing . . .

# ROUND 1
## WHO IS THIS?
Guess our podcast guests from the clues below . . .

1. He has a brother in indie rock band Suede.
   I bet Thursday is murder round at his.
   It would be pointless to give you any more clues.

2. Which of our guests wrote the best-selling political book *How Stormont Fell*?
   He also appeared in Victoria Wood's *Dinnerladies* as the host of a quiz called *Totally Trivial*.
   He was always going for gold and he was truly game for a laugh.

3. Which of our guests has portrayed Tony Blair on screen in three different TV shows?
   He has also played Kenneth Williams, David Frost, Brian Clough and Chris Tarrant.

4.  Which of our guests duetted with Dawn French for Comic Relief, lip-synching to Lizzo's song 'Juice'?
    A wedding celebration catapulted her to fame.
    I sing a song of praise when she's on my gogglebox.
5.  Which of our guests first appeared on our TV in 1962 and has performed duets with Demis Roussos and Cilla Black?
    He's a redhead and he makes our hearts go boom-boom.

# ROUND 2
## WHO IS OLDER?

We give you a pair of celebrities, and you simply have to guess who is older. Bonus mark if you get the right age gap.

1.  Who is older, Kevin Costner or Kevin Keegan?
2.  Who is older, Susan Boyle or Danny Boyle?
3.  Who is older, Kelsey Grammer or MC Hammer?
4.  Who is older, Billy Ray Cyrus or Billy Bob Thornton?
5.  Who is older, Anthea Turner or Lorraine Kelly?
6.  Who is older, Neil Diamond or Neil Young?
7.  Who is older, Matt Lucas or Noel Fielding?
8.  Who is older, Harry Connick Jr or Robert Downey Jr?
9.  Who is older, Hugh Grant or Hugh Laurie?
10. Who is older, Smokey Robinson or Anne Robinson?
11. Who is older, Harry Styles or Harry Kane?
12. Who is older, Tracey Ullman or Tracey Emin?

13. Who is older, Kevin Spacey or Kevin Bacon?
14. Who is older, John Bishop or John Barnes?
15. Who is older, Timmy Mallett or Jimmy Nail?
16. Who is older, Dominic Cummings or Dominic West?
17. Who is older, Pudsey Bear or Mr Blobby?
18. Who is older, Vernon Kay or Peter Kay?
19. Who is older, Paul Simon or Art Garfunkel?
20. Who is older, Ant or Dec?
21. Who is older, Lucy Liu or Lucy Porter?
22. Who is older, Jenny Ryan or Ryan Gosling?

# ROUND 3
## HISTORY BY DECADE

1. 1900–10
   In 1906, which northern European country was the first to grant women the vote?
2. 1910–20
   Which month of 1917 saw the Great Socialist Revolution in Russia?
3. 1920–30
   The Irish Free State was established in 1922, comprising how many of the 32 counties of Ireland?
4. 1930–40
   A civil war, fought between 1936 and 1939, which brought Francisco Franco to power, occurred in which country?

5. 1940–50

   Who became the first prime minister of Israel in 1948?

6. 1950–60

   Which agency, responsible for aeronautics and space research, was established in the USA in 1958?

7. 1960–70

   Beginning in 1967, a war was fought between the Republic of Biafra and which African country?

8. 1970–80

   In 1973, a coup in which South American country overthrew the Popular Unity government led by President Salvador Allende?

9. 1980–90

   Which prime minister of India was assassinated by her own bodyguards in 1984?

10. 1990–2000

    In December 1993, which leader of the Medellin drugs cartel was killed by special operations units of the National Police of Colombia?

# ROUND 4
## OLYMPIC SPORTS

None of these sports are scheduled to be contested at the 2024 Paris Olympics, but some of them have at some point featured in the modern Olympic Games, either as an official sport or a demonstration sport. Can you work out which ones are real Olympic sports, and which we've put in to confuse you?

1. Horse long jump
2. Tug of war
3. Ferret legging
4. Club swinging
5. Solo synchronised swimming
6. Fly fishing
7. Croquet
8. Poodle clipping
9. Squash
10. Motorboating
11. Firefighting
12. Pigeon shooting
13. Netball
14. Ski ballet
15. Grass bobsleigh

# ROUND 5
## TV AND FILM

1. On which day does the action of both *Die Hard* and *Die Hard 2* take place?
2. In Byker Grove, during which activity was the character PJ temporarily blinded?
3. Which 1981 film is the only Best Picture Oscar winner to contain all of the letters of 'Oscar' in its title?

4. On *Blind Date*, what was the name of the man who did the voiceover summaries of each contestant?

5. What was the Gladiator name of Diane Youdale?

6. In which classic film from 1939 did a man called Frank Morgan play the title character, actually quite a small part in the film?

7. Ash Ketchum is the main human character in which series of cartoons?

8. As seen in a popular disney film, what is the idiomatic Swahili translation of 'No Worries'?

9. Who were the two credited writers of *Fawlty Towers*?

10. On which show was Doctor Teeth and the Electric Mayhem the house band?

11. Which TV show has episodes including 'Cash and Curry', 'He Ain't Heavy, He's My Uncle' and 'A Slow Bus To Chingford'?

12. On the quiz show *University Challenge*, how many points do you get for correctly answering one part of a standard three-part bonus question?

13. What four words complete this phrase uttered by the character Clubber Lang in the film *Rocky III*: 'I don't hate Balboa, but _____'?

14. In which film does Michael J Fox star as a high school basketball player called Scott Howard?

15. Which 1990s TV show charted what happened to twins Brandon and Brenda Walsh after they moved from Minnesota to California?

# ROUND 6
## GENERAL KNOWLEDGE

1. What is the mix of spices used in Indian cooking that roughly translates as 'hot mix'?
2. Which MP conducted a four-year affair with John Major?
3. What name is given to a young pigeon?
4. Dublin lies on which river?
5. Who discovered penicillin?
6. The novels *Restless*, *Ordinary Thunderstorms* and *Stars and Bars* were written by whom?
7. What was the name of Elvis Presley's backing band?
8. What was the surname of Jerry and Margo in *The Good Life*?
9. Which figure skater hired a hitman to injure her rival Nancy Kerrigan before the 1994 Winter Olympics?
10. In which year was the Disney classic *101 Dalmatians* released?
11. Which UK city is served by Prestwick airport?
12. Who won the first Eurovision Song Contest in 1956?
13. Which Blondie track begins with the words 'Once I had a love and it was a gas'?
14. Which lake holds the largest volume of water in the United Kingdom?
15. Vincent David Furnier is the real name of which rock star?
16. Which chemical element has the symbol Mn?
17. The fictional school of St Trinian's was created by which cartoonist?

18.  What is the capital city of California?
19.  In the *Toy Story* films, who voices Buzz Lightyear?
20.  What is the most widely consumed meat in the world?

# ROUND 7
## GENERAL KNOWLEDGE

1.  On a standard typewriter keyboard, which letter is between V and N?
2.  The character of Dr Ian Malcolm appears in which long-running film franchise?
3.  Which member of Led Zeppelin had the nickname Bonzo?
4.  Ichthyology is the study of what?
5.  Who became the second president of the USA when George Washington retired?
6.  What is the signature red wine made from Nebbiolo grapes?
7.  Marbled white, gatekeeper and purple hairstreak are all types of what?
8.  What is the state capital of Louisiana?
9.  Which English rugby union side play their games at Twickenham Stoop?
10. What nationality was Frédéric Chopin?
11. Who is the founder of Uber?
12. Zechariah is the father of which biblical figure?
13. Convict Robert Stroud was better known as whom?

14. What was the name of Jacques Cousteau's boat?
15. How many cards are there in a tarot pack?
16. What do you get if you add a baker's dozen to a score?
17. In *Coronation Street*, what was Ken Barlow's first job?
18. In music, in what key is a piece written if its key signature shows three flats?
19. What is the name of Snoopy's brother?
20. In which British city is the railway station Temple Meads?

# ROUND 8
## GENERAL KNOWLEDGE

1. In the song 'Penny Lane', what is the pretty nurse selling?
2. In *Dad's Army*, what were Private Godfrey's sisters called?
3. In Greek mythology, what was the sword of Damocles suspended by?
4. In the British army, which rank comes between lieutenant and major?
5. In which county is Woburn Abbey?
6. Which month does Michaelmas Day fall in?
7. What was the name of Rigsby's cat in the sitcom *Rising Damp*?
8. What is the name of the yellow character in Cluedo?
9. In which sport are the Lutz and Salchow moves performed?
10. In which two cities would you find Cleopatra's Needles?
11. Which sitcom took place in the village of Cricket St Thomas?

12. Viktor Barna was a five-time world champion in which sport?

13. How many pieces of music do you get to choose on *Desert Island Discs*?

14. *Kiss Me Kate* is the musical version of which Shakespeare play?

15. Susan and Lucy visited Narnia, but who were the two brothers who went with them?

16. Andrés Segovia is associated with which instrument?

17. In which city is Heriot-Watt University?

18. The village of Anatevka is the setting for which musical?

19. St Stephen's Day is better known as what?

20. Penrod 'Penry' Pooch is better known as which cartoon character?

# ROUND 9
## GENERAL KNOWLEDGE

1. Tom Thumb, Tennis Ball and Winter Density are all types of what?

2. Was 1994 a leap year?

3. 'Up Where We Belong' was the theme tune to which film?

4. Which TV pub had a terrible fire in 1986?

5. What are Dame Edna Everage's favourite flowers?

6. Bucks Fizz won the Eurovision Song Contest in 1981 with which song?

7.   What is Postman Pat's surname?

8.   In a box of Quality Street, what colour wrapper is the coconut eclair?

9.   Which *Sesame Street* character lives in a dustbin?

10.  Which Italian pudding literally means 'pick me up'?

11.  What are the first two letters of a central Edinburgh postcode?

12.  'Live Well For Less', was a slogan for which UK supermarket?

13.  What is the name of Lennie's close companion in *Of Mice and Men*?

14.  Who appeared on the first ever cover of *Rolling Stone* magazine?

15.  Dr Henry Walton Jones Jr is better known by what name?

16.  What fish is smoked to form an Arbroath smokie?

17.  Jon Arbuckle is the owner of which famous cat?

18.  Who is the voice of Gru in the *Despicable Me* films?

19.  The Amnesty International logo features barbed wire wrapped around a what?

20.  '(Everything I Do) I Do It For You' by Bryan Adams begins with what line?

# ROUND 10
## GENERAL KNOWLEDGE

1.   What is the collective noun for a large number of owls?

2. Sarah Palin was the governor of which state?

3. Which William Thackeray novel lends its name to a global magazine?

4. Danish architect Jørn Utzon designed which Australian building?

5. What is the name of the musical based on the life of Frankie Valli and the Four Seasons?

6. What was Madonna's first UK number 1 single?

7. Who was the eldest of the Marx brothers?

8. Who is Kevin the Teenager's best friend?

9. Which classic pop song begins, 'You spurn my natural emotions, you make me feel like dirt, and I'm hurt'?

10. Which US drama was set in a family undertakers?

11. Who was the top scorer at the 1986 World Cup in Mexico?

12. Who played Brian in *The Life of Brian*?

13. Where in England might you find Osborne House and Carisbrooke Castle?

14. In the TV show *Paw Patrol*, how many dogs are in Ryder's team of pups?

15. On what island were the Bee Gees born?

16. In the Bible, Salome was the stepdaughter of whom?

17. Boss Hogg was a character in which US TV series?

18. How much is the letter K worth in a game of Scrabble?

19. How many pounds are there in a stone?

20. 1n 1999 which film became Tom Hanks' first sequel?

# ROUND 11
## GENERAL KNOWLEDGE

1. In the theme tune to *Teletubbies*, which Teletubby is mentioned first?
2. In which TV game show did contestants go 'wild in the aisles'?
3. What was Margaret Thatcher's maiden name?
4. What is the 15th letter of the alphabet?
5. What is the name of the crocodile in the film *Peter Pan*?
6. Nancy Shevell is the current wife of which musician?
7. Who was the driver of Ivor the Engine?
8. What does the A stand for in DNA?
9. In what year was the Falklands War?
10. Which of the Wombles takes his name from a city in Siberia?
11. What is the highest number on a roulette wheel?
12. Hill Valley High was the fictional school in which US film?
13. How many players are there on court in a basketball team?
14. Which 1980s pop group had hits with 'Hold Me Now' and 'Doctor Doctor'?
15. What is tennis player Pete Sampras' nickname?
16. On an Ordnance Survey map, the picture of which animal represents a zoo?
17. In which US state is Fort Knox?
18. If you were born on New Year's Day, what star sign would you be?
19. In which park does Yogi Bear live?
20. What is a female donkey called?

# ROUND 12
## GENERAL KNOWLEDGE

1. Five out of the six Village People have got what?
2. What was the maiden name of Victoria Beckham?
3. Which part was played by Ewen Bremner in the film *Trainspotting*?
4. Which nut is known as the smiling nut in Iran and the happy nut in China?
5. On which lake did Donald Campbell die?
6. Who wrote the novel *Three Men In a Boat*?
7. The town of Leominster is in which British county?
8. Who lives in a pineapple under the sea?
9. What is the first name of the Queen, previously Duchess of Cornwall?
10. The soap opera *Falcon Crest* concerned a family involved in what business?
11. In what year was Donald Trump born?
12. In bingo calling, what number is Heaven's gate?
13. Which snooker player's name is an anagram of the phrase 'rented hyphens'?
14. What is the fourth book in the *Harry Potter* series?
15. Before it was renamed as JFK airport in 1963, what was JFK airport called?
16. What is the capital of Turkey?
17. In which year did Diego Maradona score a goal with his hand in the World Cup?

18. Which is the only vitamin not found in eggs?
19. Professor Robert Langdon is the hero of which book?
20. Which dinosaur's name means 'lizard under a roof'?

# ROUND 13
## GENERAL KNOWLEDGE

1. What does the W in George W Bush stand for?
2. How many stars are there on the New Zealand flag?
3. Who is the drummer in the band Metallica?
4. What was Elvis Presley's middle name?
5. Who won the Super Bowl in 2020 and 2023?
6. The Cheviots mountain range is situated mostly in which British county?
7. What is the capital city of Alabama?
8. Rob Pilatus and Fabrice Morvan are better known as what 1980s musical group?
9. In which ocean did the *Titanic* sink?
10. What is Prince William's second name?
11. What is the largest city in Canada?
12. Who played James Bond in *For Your Eyes Only*?
13. In *Star Trek*, what colour is Mr Spock's blood?
14. What is the sixth of the Ten Commandments?
15. According to the famous nursery rhyme, who found Lucy Locket's pocket?
16. The name of which country means 'The Shallows'?

17. Baku is the lowest lying capital city in the world, but of which nation is it the capital?
18. How many children does Kris Jenner have?
19. Which city has the nicknames 'Paris of South America' and 'Queen of El Plata?
20. Which composer holds the British record for winning the most Academy Awards?

## ROUND 14
### GENERAL KNOWLEDGE

1. What is the most popular surname in China?
2. In the *High School Musical* movies, who played Troy Bolton?
3. Franck Muller and Patek Philippe both make what?
4. Who is the world's longest-serving actor in a soap opera?
5. Which soldier gave his name to a capital city and a beef dish?
6. What was the previous name of Ho Chi Minh City?
7. How many times did Elizabeth Taylor get married?
8. Which entire city in Britain is a World Heritage Site?
9. In 1981, who was the last elected MP to die in prison?
10. The word 'robot' comes from which language?
11. In the film *Castaway*, what was the volleyball called?
12. What is the first name of Professor McGonagall in the *Harry Potter* books?

13. Who wrote the poem *The Lady of Shalott*?
14. Which actress played Polly Sherman in the sitcom *Fawlty Towers*?
15. What is the national bird of India?
16. The actor Dave Lamb narrates which popular television show?
17. In which UK city would you find the Crucible Theatre?
18. Which adventure story starts at the Admiral Benbow inn?
19. Who wrote the 1955 novel *Lolita*?
20. The adjective vespine relates to which creature?

# ROUND 15
## GENERAL KNOWLEDGE

1. Who played Captain Hook in the 1991 film *Hook*?
2. Which political party does former New York mayor Bill de Blasio represent?
3. In the British version of Monopoly, which thoroughfare completes a set with Fleet Street and Trafalgar Square?
4. The River Danube flows into which sea?
5. An early version of which sport was known as 'mintonette' before it took its current name?
6. In which century was Heinz Tomato Ketchup first produced?
7. From which language do we get the word 'cookie'?
8. Which port has been the temporary capital of Yemen since 2015?

9. A genus of which animal is named after Richard Dawkins?
10. Which is the only inanimate sign of the zodiac?
11. Which Oasis song opens with the words 'Today is gonna be the day'?
12. The Baggies is the nickname of which English football club?
13. In which city was the *Titanic* built?
14. Liberty City, Vice City and San Andreas are cities in which video game series?
15. Bucatini is a type of which food?
16. Which is the largest cathedral in the UK?
17. In the film *Saving Private Ryan*, who played Private Ryan?
18. In *Sesame Street*, what is the name of Bert's roommate?
19. What was the title of the Beatles' first studio album, released in 1963?
20. What is Scotland's second highest mountain?

# ROUND 16
## GENERAL KNOWLEDGE

1. Which Mark Ronson song was the biggest selling single of 2015?
2. What does the I stand for in the acronym FYI?
3. Which London hotel was the first in the world to offer a private bathroom to each guest?
4. What was the name of Sherlock Holmes' landlady?
5. The mojito cocktail originated in which country?

6. Who was the Labour Home Secretary between June 2001 and December 2004?

7. How many sides are there on a heptadecagon?

8. Which spirit's name when translated into English means 'little water'?

9. Which London Underground line has the most stations?

10. John Travolta played which character in the film *Pulp Fiction*?

11. Meadowhall shopping centre is in which English city?

12. Who was president of the USA at the coronation of Queen Elizabeth II?

13. Who is older, Bernie Taupin or Elton John?

14. Which Charles Dickens novel features the characters John Harmon and Bella Wilfer?

15. The Aidensfield Arms was a pub in which TV series?

16. The mutineers from HMS *Bounty* settled on which island?

17. Who played Samuel Johnson in the sitcom *Blackadder the Third*?

18. Who was the author of the *Paddington* books?

19. How many times did Pete Sampras win the Wimbledon men's singles title?

20. What is 15 per cent of 2,000?

# ROUND 17
## GENERAL KNOWLEDGE

1. Who is the alter ego of Sir Percy Blakeney?
2. Who was the first ever winner of *Britain's Got Talent*?
3. How many furlongs are there in a mile?
4. In which city was Terry Waite kidnapped in 1987?
5. Which Queen song features the lyrics 'Caviar and cigarettes, well versed in etiquette'?
6. Which year did Channel 4 begin transmission in the UK?
7. How many players are there on a curling team?
8. Daniel Negreanu, Phil Ivey and Stephen Chidwick are famous players of which game?
9. Which is taller, Westminster Abbey or St Paul's Cathedral?
10. If you have the letters MRCVS after your name, what is your profession?
11. Who wrote the novel *The Curious Incident of the Dog in the Night-Time*?
12. What is the fifth letter of the Greek alphabet?
13. Who had a UK hit in 1960 with 'My Old Man's a Dustman'?
14. The city of Portsmouth is in which English county?
15. Touchstone is a character in which Shakespeare play?
16. Who is the only Spice Girl actually named after a spice?
17. Rebecca Rabbit and Dr Brown Bear are characters from which television show?
18. Who killed Lee Harvey Oswald?

19. Nancy Cartwright provides the voice of which cartoon character?

20. Which book begins with the line 'It was a bright cold day in April, and the clocks were striking thirteen'?

# ROUND 18
## GENERAL KNOWLEDGE

1. Who is the creator of the cartoon cat, Garfield?
2. Which element has the chemical symbol Ni?
3. In which year was Prince George of Cambridge born?
4. In which US state is Alcatraz?
5. Which 1984 pop song begins 'I made it through the wilderness'?
6. Who played Lord Brett Sinclair in the TV series *The Persuaders*?
7. What is the last sign of the zodiac alphabetically?
8. Who hosts the ITV quiz *Tenable*?
9. Who was older, Don Everly or Phil Everly?
10. The sitcom *Dad's Army* was written by which two writers?
11. How many marzipan balls should there be on a simnel cake?
12. In the British version of Monopoly, how much would it cost you to buy the property Mayfair?
13. What musical aid was invented in 1711 by trumpeter John Shore?

14. Which is the largest country in the world with only four letters in its name?
15. Who played Lucius Malfoy in the *Harry Potter* film series?
16. Which river flows through the city of Durham?
17. Who directed the film *Easy Rider* in 1969?
18. What was the name of the first space shuttle?
19. Who provided the voice of the Cadbury's Caramel Bunny?
20. What was the capital of England before London?

# ROUND 19
## GENERAL KNOWLEDGE

1. Which band performed the theme tune to the sitcom *Friends*?
2. Who played the title role in the film *Carrie*?
3. Stem, straight and lazy daisy are all types of what?
4. In *The Wizard of Oz*, what is Dorothy's surname?
5. What is the first name of TV barrister Judge Rinder?
6. The name of which electromechanical horn comes from the Greek for 'I shriek'?
7. Dr Peter Venkman is a character in which supernatural film?
8. Tivoli Gardens, the Amalienborg Palace and Frederik's Church can be found in which capital city?
9. In which Shakespeare play do Benedick and Don Pedro appear?
10. Which sea does the River Thames empty into?

11. What official documents, costing 37½ pence each, were abolished in 1987?
12. How many dots are there on a six-sided dice?
13. Which sport is the subject of the film *Field of Dreams*?
14. What was the name of the holiday camp in the sitcom *Hi-de-Hi*?
15. Which is the most populated state in the USA?
16. Do stalactites grow up or down?
17. Ant and Dec starred in which sci-fi comedy film in 2006?
18. Which alcoholic drink translates into English as 'hunting master'?
19. Who was the original host of the UK game show *The Price Is Right*?
20. Alton Towers theme park is in which English county?

# ROUND 20
## GENERAL KNOWLEDGE

1. Which British football team is based at Tynecastle Park?
2. Which is the last-named capital city alphabetically?
3. Which British prime minister was known by the nickname 'Honest Stan'?
4. How many months of the year have exactly 30 days?
5. What is the national language of Liechtenstein?
6. In which month is the Chelsea Flower Show held?
7. Which sci-fi hero has a girlfriend called Dale Arden?

8. Who is Geraldine Granger better known as?
9. What is Harper Lee's second novel?
10. Who voices Montgomery Burns in *The Simpsons*?
11. In which year did Prince Charles marry Camilla Parker Bowles?
12. Which long-serving ex Labour MP was known as 'The Beast of Bolsover'?
13. In which year did India gain independence from Britain?
14. What is the only film and sequel to win Best Picture Oscars?
15. Which UK railway station has the most platforms?
16. Which Teletubby is the tallest?
17. In which city is the show *Frasier* set?
18. Who won the BAFTA for Best Leading Actor for his role in *Wolf Hall*?
19. What was the name of the butler in *The Addams Family*?
20. What did George W Bush choke on in 2003, causing him to briefly lose consciousness?

# ROUND 21
## GENERAL KNOWLEDGE

1. The Mysterons were the enemy of whom?
2. Who is the only Blue Peter presenter to have been sacked?
3. What does the DC in Washington, DC stand for?
4. Where was the first Butlin's holiday camp built?
5. Who wrote the books *Ratburger* and *Billionaire Boy*?

6. Who succeeded Peter Davison as Doctor Who?

7. What breed of dog is used to advertise Hush Puppies?

8. Eton College is in which county?

9. Which country won the FIFA World Cup in 1970, 1994 and 2002?

10. The Boswells were the family in which TV comedy?

11. Which chemical element has the symbol As?

12. In which English county is Tatton Park?

13. What does a red triangle represent on an Ordnance Survey map?

14. What animal is found on the Alfa Romeo logo?

15. Who is older, Richard Gere or Richard Branson?

16. A crash is a collective noun for which group of animals?

17. The music 'By the Sleepy Lagoon' is the theme tune to which popular show?

18. What is the longest river in Europe?

19. The Spanish word *amarillo* translates to what in English?

20. Who plays Cat in *Red Dwarf*?

# ROUND 22
## GENERAL KNOWLEDGE

1. What was the name of the captain of the *Titanic*?

2. In cockney vernacular, how much money is a monkey?

3. Which band had a hit in 1979 with 'Day Trip to Bangor'?

4. In the Isle of Man TT races, what does TT actually stand for?

5. In which 1997 film does John Travolta play an angel?

6. Who was the first character to appear on *EastEnders*?

7. Which architect designed The Shard in London?

8. Who succeeded Paddy Ashdown as leader of the Liberal Democrats in 1999?

9. Which boxer had part of his ear bitten off by Mike Tyson in 1997?

10. What are the first names of Harry Potter's parents?

11. In the film *The Great Escape,* what are the names of the three tunnels dug by the prisoners?

12. What game starts with a squidge off?

13. What is the surname of the British singer Adele?

14. In which English county is Camber Sands beach?

15. What is the largest country in the world to have only one time zone?

16. Which famous American writer has also published novels under the name Richard Bachman?

17. How many keys are there on a standard piano?

18. Which is the only American state with a 'z' in its name?

19. What was Spike Milligan's real first name?

20. Who are the two elderly hecklers who sit in the balcony at the Muppet Theatre?

## ROUND 23
## GENERAL KNOWLEDGE

1. By what name is the Gravelly Hill Interchange better known?
2. In the *Wallace and Gromit* animated series, what colour is Wallace's tank top?
3. Billy Corgan is the lead singer of which band?
4. In the game of Cluedo, which weapon comes first alphabetically?
5. After how many years would you celebrate your crystal wedding anniversary?
6. Who played Captain Stephen Peacock in *Are You Being Served?*
7. In which year did a woman first win a Best Director Oscar?
8. Which character did Susan Sarandon play in the 1991 film: Thelma or Louise?
9. In which year was the Gunpowder Plot?
10. In the building product MDF, what does MDF stand for?
11. What would you be served with if ordering 'cluck and grunt' in an American diner?
12. Jackson is the capital of which US state?
13. What is the name of the dog in the *Famous Five* novels?
14. Which was the last song to be released by the band Queen before Freddie Mercury's death?
15. In which year did the Queen celebrate her silver jubilee?
16. Which of these US presidents was born first: John F Kennedy, Richard Nixon or Ronald Reagan?

17. What fruit is used to make the liqueur Calvados?

18. Who was the first winner of the BBC Sports Personality of the Year Award in 1954?

19. Who had a number one hit in 1985 with '19'?

# ROUND 24
## GENERAL KNOWLEDGE

1. Simon May and Leslie Osborne composed which famous British television theme tune in 1984?

2. Which South American country is bordered by Colombia to the north and Peru to the east and south?

3. Who played Carla Tortelli in the sitcom *Cheers*?

4. Which US president's signature is on a plaque on the moon?

5. Who drives the school bus in *The Simpsons*?

6. Captain Sensible sang the theme tune to which UK TV game show?

7. The band Duran Duran are named after a character in which 1968 science-fiction film?

8. Which metropolitan area in the Pearl River Delta has a name that literally translates from Cantonese as 'fragrant harbour'?

9. How many legs does a scorpion have?

10. Benedict Cumberbatch plays mathematician Alan Turing in which 2014 film?

11. Federation Square and Flinders Street railway station can be found in which Australian city?
12. What is the medical name for the shin bone?
13. Which national cricket team are known as 'The Black Caps'?
14. Who wrote the 1962 novel *One Flew Over the Cuckoo's Nest*?
15. Which male name is sometimes used as a nickname for the autopilot of an aeroplane?
16. Which instrument did jazz legend Artie Shaw play?
17. Which of the Beatles is dressed in white on the cover of the *Abbey Road* album?
18. What do the two 'M's stand for in the sweet brand M&Ms?
19. Who was older, Eric Morecambe or Ernie Wise?
20. Which pop star visited Britain in 2001 to address the Oxford Union on the subject of child welfare?

# ROUND 25
## ANCIENT OR MODERN

This may remind you of the 'Highbrow Lowbrow' round in *House of Games*, but it's different, honest. There are two questions, one of which relates to something from the past, one of which is much more up to date. Your contestants can choose whether to take a history question or a modern question. Or you could just give them both to make it a bit easier.

1a. What was the surname of the late 18th- and early 19th-century scientist who invented the smallpox vaccine?

1b. What is the surname of Kim Kardashian's mother?

2a. What name was shared by the mother and daughter of King Henry I? His daughter ruled over much of south-west England in the 1140s.

2b. Which stage musical was released as a movie in 2022 and starred Lashana Lynch as a teacher?

3a. What was the surname of the 16th-century explorer who sailed on a galleon named the *Golden Hind*?

3b. Which Canadian rapper is best known for songs like 'What's My Name' and 'Hotline Bling'?

4a. In Norse mythology, what is the name for a foretold catastrophic event known as 'The doom of the Gods'?

4b. What is the name of the 2017 Marvel movie directed by Taika Waititi and starring Chris Hemsworth?

5a. What was the first name of the British prime minister whose surname was Perceval and who was assassinated in 1812?

5b. What is the first name of the *Made in Chelsea* star whose surname is Matthews and who is married to Vogue Williams?

## FINAL ROUND
### WIPEOUT / GRAND FINAL

To add a bit of jeopardy to the end of your quiz, it's great to have a round where people can win and lose a lot of points.

This round can either be a total wipeout – put a wrong answer and your round score is zero (blank answers do not count). Or you get +1 for a correct answer, –1 for an incorrect answer and 0 for a blank/crossed out answer (keeps it tense).

1. Which English county has a name literally meaning 'People of the North'?

2. Brass is an alloy of copper and which other metal?

3. 'Your mother has a smooth forehead' is one of the ultimate insults in which language?

4. What is the largest key on all standard computer keyboards?

5. Iran broke off diplomatic relations with Great Britain in 1989 because of the publication of which book?

6. Which patron saint is shared by Canada, Ethiopia, Georgia, Greece, Montenegro, Portugal, Serbia and Russia among others?

7. Which game can be played under the Regency Rules which state that 'the Nash Convention allows superseding after parallel moves, and all Terraces . . . are wild, unless of course you are in Spoon'?

8. In pre-decimal currency, how many old pence were there to the pound?

9. If you spell out the names of all the numbers from one up to one hundred, which number comes last in alphabetical order?

10. What is the only square on a standard London Monopoly board to contain all the letters of the word 'Monopoly'?

# EXTRA QUESTIONS

1. As far as can be known from the story, what nationality is Jack from 'Jack and the Beanstalk'?
2. What is the only country in the world with a name in English ending in H?
3. What name is given in France to the day before Ash Wednesday?
4. How many letters of the alphabet are not used in the names of any of the months of the year in English?

# Answers

## CHAPTER 1

### GENERAL KNOWLEDGE
1. Edward VIII – abdicated in favour of George VI
2. Louis Braille
3. George Washington, Abraham Lincoln, Thomas Jefferson, Theodore Roosevelt
4. New Zealand
5. A loganberry
6. The British Museum
7. The Hairy Bikers
8. The Adriatic Sea
9. A gaggle
10. The structure of DNA
11. Milan Kundera
12. The Great Pyramid of Giza
13. Tim Rice
14. Tupac Shakur
15. Carmela
16. Ben Johnson
17. Marion Crane
18. Roald Amundsen

19. Regent's Park
20. Officer Crabtree

# CHAPTER 2

## *PUZZLING*
3

## *BLOCKBUSTERS*
1. Sophomore
2. Australia
3. New Zealand
4. Television
5. Alan Partridge
6. Crosswords
7. Lithium
8. Accrington Stanley
9. Um Bongo
10. *Succession*

## *ASK THE FAMILY*
Brainteaser: £8 and £4

## *FAMILY FORTUNES*

| | |
|---|---|
| Name something you wouldn't try even once | Sex on a train |
| Name something the dentist says | Just a small prick |
| Name something everyone has more than two of on their body | Arms |
| Name something that comes in sevens | Fingers |
| Name a bird with a long neck | Naomi Campbell |
| Name something a car has more than 2 of | Wheels |
| Name something accociated with The Three Bears | Red Riding Hood |
| Name something your partner can't manage without | Sex |
| Name something you close | Legs |
| Name something associated with Alice in Wonderland | The Tin Man |

## ANSWERS ☑

**FOR THE OLDER PEOPLE**

1a. Brown, Columbia, Cornell, Dartmouth, Harvard, Princeton, University of Pennsylvania, Yale
1b. Alaska, Washington, Oregon, California, Hawaii
1c. Sunak, Truss, May, Brown, Blair, Major, Heath, Eden (then Wilson, Attlee, Baldwin, Asquith)
2a. Austria, Czech Republic, Hungary, Luxembourg, Slovakia
2b. 1901 (Victoria), 1910 (Edward VII), 1936 (George V), 1952 (George VI)
3a. a) Herbivore b) Carnivore c) Carnivore
3b. a) Not b) Apostrophe c) Not
4a. a) 1995 b) 1984
4b. a) 1987 b) 1996
5. They contain the same number of letters in the word as the number itself
(Spanish: five = cinco; English: four = four; German: four = vier; Italian: three = tre)

**FOR THE YOUNGER PEOPLE**

1a. Mercury, Venus, Earth, Mars, Jupiter, Saturn, Uranus, Neptune
1b. Asia, Africa, Europe, North America, South America, Australia, Antarctica
2a. London, Edinburgh, Cardiff, Belfast
2b. North, South, East, West
3a. a) *Star Wars* b) Marvel c) Marvel
3b. a) UK b) US c) UK
4a. a) Marie Curie b) Charles Darwin
4b. a) Taylor Swift b) Harry Styles
5. Nine

## CHAPTER 3
### COUNTDOWN

1. Lethargic
2. Betrothal
3. Loathsome
4. Goodnight
5. Shameless
6. Roadblock
7. Molecular
8. Abolishes
9. Breakfast
10. Consulate

## CHAPTER 4
### SPORT

1. Horse racing
2. Adidas
3. Cross-country skiing and rifle shooting
4. Judo
5. Rugby union
6. Table tennis
7. Swimming
8. Browns
9. Boxing
10. Trampolining
11. Badminton
12. Bobsleigh
13. Jayne Torvill and Christopher Dean
14. High jump
15. OJ Simpson
16. Swimming
17. Ice hockey
18. Baseball

19. Curling
20. Polo

# CHAPTER 5

## SCREEN TEST

Vinnie Jones, Paul
Gascoigne

# CHAPTER 6

## MUSIC

1. 'Goodbye Yellow Brick Road' – Elton John
2. 'Gangnam Style' – Psy
3. 'Comfortably Numb' – Pink Floyd
4. 'R.E.S.P.E.C.T.' – Aretha Franklin
5. 'Karma Chameleon' – Culture Club
6. 'St Elmo's Fire' (Man in Motion) – John Parr
7. 'Trapped' – Colonel Abrams8.    Hakuna Matata
8. 'The Great (Grate) Pretender' – The Platters / Freddie Mercury
9. 'I Still Haven't Found What I'm Looking For' – U2
10. 'Letter From America' – The Proclaimers
11. 'Stairway to Heaven' – Led Zeppelin (will also accept 'ThreeSteps to Heaven' by Eddie Cochran although that was released in 1960)
12. 'Orinoco Flow' – Enya
13. 'Itsy Bitsy Teeny Weeny Yellow Polka Dot Bikini' – Bombalurina in 1990 (or many others)
14. 'Kinky Boots' – Patrick Macnee and Honor Blackman
15. 'Pump Up the Jam' – Technotronic

## CHAPTER 7
### *WHO WANTS TO BE A MILLIONAIRE?*

1. JFK
2. Rapunzel
3. Ronseal
4. *Breaking Bad*
5. Irish setter
6. Congress
7. Feed dog
8. Hellmann's (Heinz 1869, Hellmann's 1913, Colman's 1814, Lea and Perrins 1837)
9. Sikhism
10. Burping
11. Muscles
12. Argentina
13. Architecture
14. Australia
15. World War II

## CHAPTER 8
### MEAN QUIZ

1. All of them (an annoying answer but technically true)
2. Paul (his first name is James)
3. Antarctica (the Sahara is the largest hot desert)
4. Vatican City (a perfectly obvious answer, but again, it does annoy people)
5. Neither (it doesn't have a brain or a heart)
6. Brazil (French Guiana is legally part of France)

# CHAPTER 9
## JET SET
### Town
1. Bath
2. Shropshire
3. Gateshead
4. Lincolnshire
5. Taunton
6. Weatherfield
7. Tobermory
8. Douglas
9. Ontario
10. Tripoli
11. Nougat
12. Milton Keynes

### Country
1. East Pakistan
2. Jamaica
3. New Zealand
4. Malaysia
5. Rwanda
6. Ethiopia
7. Zambia
8. Vietnam
9. Portugal
10. Italy
11. Lithuania
12. Spain
13. Australia
14. Czech Republic
15. Indonesia
16. Egypt

## SUPER QUIZ
## ROUND 1
### WHO IS THIS?
1. Richard Osman
2. Henry Kelly
3. Michael Sheen
4. Kate Bottley
5. Basil Brush

## ROUND 2
### WHO IS OLDER?
1. Kevin Keegan, by four years
2. Danny Boyle, by four years
3. Kelsey Grammer, by seven years
4. Billy Bob Thornton, by six years
5. Lorraine Kelly, by six months
6. Neil Diamond, by five years
7. Noel Fielding, by one year
8. Robert Downey Jr, by two years
9. Hugh Laurie, by one year
10. Smokey Robinson, by four years
11. Harry Kane by one year
12. Tracey Ullman, by three years
13. Kevin Bacon, by one year
14. John Barnes, by three years
15. Jimmy Nail, by one year
16. Dominic West, by three years
17. Pudsey Bear, by seven years
18. Peter Kay, by one year
19. Paul Simon, by 23 days
20. Dec, by 54 days
21. Lucy Liu, by four years
22. Ryan Gosling, by two years

# ROUND 3

## HISTORY BY DECADE

1. Finland
2. October
3. 26
4. Spain
5. David Ben-Gurion
6. NASA (National Aeronautics and Space Administration)
7. Nigeria
8. Chile
9. Indira Gandhi
10. Pablo Escobar

# ROUND 4

## OLYMPIC SPORTS

1. Horse long jump: YES (discontinued)
2. Tug of war: YES (discontinued)
3. Ferret legging: NO (never included)
4. Club swinging: YES (discontinued)
5. Solo synchronised swimming: YES (discontinued)
6. Fly fishing: NO (never included)
7. Croquet: YES (discontinued)
8. Poodle clipping: NO (never included, but someone printed an April Fool's Day hoax saying that it had featured in the 1900 Olympics, and the lie caught on)
9. Squash: NO (never included)
10. Motorboating: YES (discontinued)
11. Firefighting: YES (demonstration)
12. Pigeon shooting: YES (demonstration)
13. Netball: NO (never included)
14. Ski ballet: YES (demonstration)
15. Grass bobsleigh: NO (never included)

# ROUND 5
## TV AND FILM
1. Christmas Eve
2. Paintballing
3. *Chariots of Fire*
4. Our Graham (Graham Skidmore)
5. Jet
6. *The Wizard of Oz*
7. Pokémon
8. Hakuna Matata
9. John Cleese and Connie Booth
10. *The Muppet Show*
11. *Only Fools and Horses*
12. Five
13. I pity the fool
14. *Teen Wolf*
15. *Beverly Hills 90210*

# ROUND 6
## GENERAL KNOWLEDGE
1. Garam masala
2. Edwina Currie
3. A squab
4. The Liffey
5. Alexander Fleming
6. William Boyd
7. The Jordanaires
8. Leadbetter
9. Tonya Harding
10. 1961
11. Glasgow
12. Switzerland

13. 'Heart of Glass'
14. Loch Ness
15. Alice Cooper
16. Manganese
17. Ronald Searle
18. Sacramento
19. Tim Allen
20. Pork

# ROUND 7
## GENERAL KNOWLEDGE

1. B
2. *Jurassic Park*
3. John Bonham
4. Fish
5. John Adams
6. Barolo
7. Butterfly
8. Baton Rouge
9. Harlequins
10. Polish
11. Travis Kalanick
12. John the Baptist
13. The Birdman of Alcatraz
14. *Calypso*
15. 78
16. 33
17. Teacher
18. E flat
19. Spike
20. Bristol

## ROUND 8
### GENERAL KNOWLEDGE
1. Poppies
2. Dolly and Cissy
3. A single horse hair
4. Captain
5. Bedfordshire
6. September
7. Vienna
8. Colonel Mustard
9. Figure skating
10. London and New York
11. *To the Manor Born*
12. Table tennis
13. Eight
14. *The Taming of the Shrew*
15. Peter and Edmund
16. Guitar
17. Edinburgh
18. *Fiddler on the Roof*
19. Boxing Day
20. Hong Kong Phooey

## ROUND 9
### GENERAL KNOWLEDGE
1. Lettuce
2. No
3. *An Officer and a Gentleman*
4. The Rover's Return
5. Gladioli
6. 'Making Your Mind Up'
7. Clifton

8. Blue
9. Oscar the Grouch
10. Tiramisu
11. EH
12. Sainsbury's
13. George
14. John Lennon
15. Indiana Jones
16. Haddock
17. Garfield
18. Steve Carell
19. Candle
20. 'Look into my eyes'

# ROUND 10

## GENERAL KNOWLEDGE

1. A parliament
2. Alaska
3. *Vanity Fair*
4. Sydney Opera House
5. *The Jersey Boys*
6. 'Into the Groove'
7. Chico
8. Perry
9. 'Ever Fallen in Love' by Buzzcocks
10. *Six Feet Under*
11. Gary Lineker
12. Graham Chapman
13. Isle of Wight
14. Six – Marshall, Rubble, Rocky, Zuma, Chase and Skye.
15. Isle of Man
16. Herod
17. *The Dukes of Hazzard*

18. Five points
19. 14
20. *Toy Story 2*

# ROUND 11
## GENERAL KNOWLEDGE

1. Tinky Winky
2. *Supermarket Sweep*
3. Roberts
4. O
5. Tick Tock
6. Paul McCartney
7. Jones the Steam
8. Acid
9. 1982
10. Tomsk
11. 36
12. *Back to the Future*
13. Five
14. Thompson Twins
15. Pistol Pete
16. Elephant
17. Kentucky
18. Capricorn
19. Jellystone National Park
20. A jenny

# ROUND 12
## GENERAL KNOWLEDGE

1. Moustaches
2. Adams
3. Spud
4. Pistachio
5. Coniston Water

6.  Jerome K Jerome
7.  Herefordshire
8.  SpongeBob SquarePants
9.  Camilla
10. Wine production
11. 1946
12. 78
13. Stephen Hendry
14. *Harry Potter and the Goblet of Fire*
15. Idlewild
16. Ankara
17. 1986
18. Vitamin C
19. *The Da Vinci Code*
20. Stegosaurus

# ROUND 13

## GENERAL KNOWLEDGE

1.  Walker
2.  Four
3.  Lars Ulrich
4.  Aaron
5.  Kansas City Chiefs
6.  Northumberland
7.  Montgomery
8.  Milli Vanilli
9.  North Atlantic
10. Arthur
11. Toronto
12. Roger Moore
13. Green
14. Thou shalt not kill
15. Kitty Fisher
16. The Bahamas

17. Azerbaijan
18. Six
19. Buenos Aires
20. John Barry

## ROUND 14

### GENERAL KNOWLEDGE

1. Wang
2. Zac Efron
3. Watches
4. William Roache
5. Wellington
6. Saigon
7. Eight
8. Bath
9. Bobby Sands
10. Czech
11. Wilson
12. Minerva
13. Alfred, Lord Tennyson
14. Connie Booth
15. Peacock
16. *Come Dine with Me*
17. Sheffield
18. *Treasure Island*
19. Vladimir Nabokov
20. Wasp

## ROUND 15

### GENERAL KNOWLEDGE

1. Dustin Hoffman
2. Democrats

3. The Strand
4. Black Sea
5. Volleyball
6. 19th (1876)
7. Dutch
8. Aden
9. Fish
10. Libra
11. 'Wonderwall'
12. West Bromwich Albion
13. Belfast
14. *Grand Theft Auto*
15. Pasta
16. Liverpool Cathedral
17. Matt Damon
18. Ernie
19. *Please Please Me*
20. Ben Macdui

# ROUND 16

## GENERAL KNOWLEDGE
1. 'Uptown Funk'
2. Information
3. The Ritz
4. Mrs Hudson
5. Cuba
6. David Blunkett
7. 17
8. Vodka
9. District Line (60)
10. Vincent Vega
11. Sheffield
12. Dwight D Eisenhower

13.  Elton John, by three years
14.  *Our Mutual Friend*
15.  *Heartbeat*
16.  Pitcairn Island
17.  Robbie Coltrane
18.  Michael Bond
19.  Seven
20.  300

## ROUND 17
### GENERAL KNOWLEDGE

1.  The Scarlet Pimpernel
2.  Paul Potts
3.  Eight
4.  Beirut
5.  'Killer Queen'
6.  1982
7.  Four
8.  Poker
9.  St Paul's at 111 metres (Westminster Abbey is a puny 69 metres)
10.  A vet (a member of the Royal College of Veterinary Surgeons)
11.  Mark Haddon
12.  Epsilon
13.  Lonnie Donegan
14.  Hampshire
15.  *As You Like It*
16.  Ginger
17.  *Peppa Pig*
18.  Jack Ruby
19.  Bart Simpson
20.  *1984* by George Orwell

# ROUND 18

## GENERAL KNOWLEDGE

1. Jim Davis
2. Nickel
3. 2013
4. California
5. 'Like a Virgin' by Madonna
6. Roger Moore
7. Virgo
8. Warwick Davis
9. Don Everly, by two years
10. Jimmy Perry and David Croft
11. 11 (to represent the 12 disciples minus Judas)
12. £400
13. Tuning fork
14. Iran
15. Jason Isaacs
16. River Wear
17. Dennis Hopper
18. Columbia
19. Miriam Margolyes
20. Winchester

# ROUND 19

## GENERAL KNOWLEDGE

1. The Rembrandts
2. Sissy Spacek
3. Sewing stitch
4. Gale
5. Robert
6. Klaxon
7. *Ghostbusters*

8. Copenhagen
9. *Much Ado About Nothing*
10. North Sea
11. Dog licences
12. 21
13. Baseball
14. Maplins
15. California
16. Down
17. *Alien Autopsy*
18. Jägermeister
19. Leslie Crowther
20. Staffordshire

## ROUND 20

### GENERAL KNOWLEDGE
1. Heart of Midlothian (Hearts)
2. Zagreb, Croatia
3. Stanley Baldwin
4. Four (April, June, September and November)
5. German
6. May
7. Flash Gordon
8. The Vicar of Dibley
9. *Go Set a Watchman*
10. Harry Shearer
11. 2005
12. Dennis Skinner
13. 1947
14. *The Godfather* and *The Godfather Part II*
15. Waterloo
16. Tinky Winky
17. Seattle

18. Mark Rylance
19. Lurch
20. A pretzel

# ROUND 21

## GENERAL KNOWLEDGE

1. Captain Scarlet
2. Richard Bacon
3. District of Columbia
4. Skegness
5. David Walliams
6. Colin Baker
7. Basset hound
8. Berkshire
9. Brazil
10. *Bread*
11. Arsenic
12. Cheshire
13. Youth hostel
14. A snake
15. Richard Gere, by one year
16. Rhinoceroses
17. *Desert Island Discs*
18. River Volga
19. Yellow
20. Danny John-Jules

# ROUND 22

## GENERAL KNOWLEDGE

1. Edward Smith
2. £500
3. Fiddler's Dram

4. Tourist Trophy
5. *Michael*
6. Den Watts
7. Renzo Piano
8. Charles Kennedy
9. Evander Holyfield
10. James and Lily
11. Tom, Dick and Harry
12. Tiddlywinks
13. Adkins
14. East Sussex
15. China
16. Stephen King
17. 88
18. Arizona
19. Terence
20. Statler and Waldorf

# ROUND 23

## GENERAL KNOWLEDGE

1. Spaghetti Junction
2. Green
3. The Smashing Pumpkins
4. Candlestick
5. 15
6. Frank Thornton
7. 2009 (Kathyrn Bigelow)
8. Louise
9. 1605
10. Medium-density fibreboard
11. Bacon and eggs
12. Mississippi
13. Timmy

14. 'The Show Must Go On'
15. 1977
16. Ronald Reagan, in 1911
17. Apples
18. Chris Chataway
19. Paul Hardcastle

# ROUND 24
## GENERAL KNOWLEDGE
1. *EastEnders*
2. Ecuador
3. Rhea Perlman
4. Richard Nixon
5. Otto
6. *Big Break*
7. *Barbarella*
8. Hong Kong
9. Eight
10. *The Imitation Game*
11. Melbourne
12. Tibia
13. New Zealand
14. Ken Kesey
15. George
16. Clarinet
17. John Lennon
18. Mars and Murrie
19. Ernie Wise, by six months
20. Michael Jackson

## ☑ FINGERS ON BUZZERS

## ROUND 25
### ANCIENT OR MODERN
1. JENNER
2. MATILDA
3. DRAKE
4. (Thor:) RAGNAROK
5. SPENCER

## FINAL ROUND
### WIPEOUT / GRAND FINAL
1. Norfolk
2. Zinc
3. Klingon
4. Space bar
5. *The Satanic Verses* (by Salman Rushdie)
6. St George (giveaway with Georgia . . . the clue is in the question)
7. Mornington Crescent
8. 240
9. Two
10. Electric Company

## EXTRA QUESTIONS
1. English (fee-fi-fo-fum, I smell the blood of an Englishman)
2. Bangladesh
3. Mardi Gras
4. Five (K, Q, W, X, Z)

# Acknowledgements

There's just one last question in this book:

Who are Lucy and Jenny hugely grateful to for their help in making this book happen?

A huge shout out to our producer – the radio and podcasting legend that is Amanda Redman. She is, as Jim Bowen would have said, 'super, smashing, great'.

To our fabulous editor, Ciara Lloyd who has been as kind, patient and supportive with us as Ben Shepherd is with the contestants on *Tipping Point*.

To our brilliant literary agent, Bev James. Thanks to Bev, Tom and the rest of the team. Like Susie Dent on *Countdown*, you've always been in our corner.

We are also awarding star prizes to:
The rest of the team from Bonnier, especially Ellie Carr and Beth Whitelaw.

Our great copy editor, Ian Greensill.

Morwenna Loughman for kicking the whole thing off.

Debi Allen, Ruth Morrison and Craig Latto.